IMAGES
of America

BRIDGEPORT ON THE SOUND

Mary K. Witkowski and Bruce Williams

ISBN 978-1-5316-0532-2

Published by Arcadia Publishing
Charleston, South Carolina

Library of Congress Catalog Card Number: 2001089155

For all general information contact Arcadia Publishing at:
Telephone 843-853-2070
Fax 843-853-0044
E-mail sales@arcadiapublishing.com
For customer service and orders:
Toll-Free 1-888-313-2665

Visit us on the Internet at www.arcadiapublishing.com

This view of Bridgeport Harbor was taken from *Picturesque America* (1874), edited by William Cullen Bryant. One passage in *Picturesque America* offers this description: "Bridgeport has been a city about forty years, and has a present estimated population of more than twenty thousand souls. It is a place of great enterprise and thrift in manufactures, foremost of which are the sewing machine works, manufacture of arms, cartridges, brass and steel wares, carriages, and water-proof fabrics, giving the profitable employment to thousands, and adding rapidly to the wealth of the place."

Contents

Acknowledgments

The authors would like to thank the following individuals who helped to inspire and guide us as we completed this book: Colin Williams, who helped type and edit the manuscript; Marley Williams, who assisted in typing; Kaye, for his knowledge and stories of the old Bridgeport waterfront; Roseanne Mansfield, Luis Rodriquez, and Elizabeth Van Tuyl of the Historical Collections Department at Bridgeport Public Library, for their incredible help in finding photographs and research materials—thanks for your wonderful assistance; Charles Brilvitch, who can rattle off Bridgeport history before the questions are asked—thanks for your generosity in freely sharing your great knowledge; John Kochiss, who continues to assist the Historical Collections Department and the Dundon House with sea facts, humor, and chocolate; Mike Bielawa and Bernie Crowley, for their knowledge of Newfield Park and James O'Rourke; the Fairfield Historical Society, for their assistance in research; Rob Sullivan, editor, and Brad Durrell, former editor of the *Bridgeport News*, for their support with the weekly column "From the Historical Collections Department;" Michael Golrick, city librarian, and Ann Osbon, assistant city librarian, Bridgeport Public Library, for allowing us to use the Historical Collections Department and the Bridgeport Public Library; and to both of our families and all of our friends, for their encouragement in our project.

The majority of photographs in this volume are from the Historical Collections Department, Bridgeport Public Library, the Dundon House Museum, and Corbit Studios. Collections that have loaned us photographs are the Fairfield Historical Society, New Haven Colony Historical Society, and the Connecticut Post. We would also like to thank the following individuals for sharing their photographs with us: Dorothy DeWalt, Jill Williams, David Barbour, Kaye Williams, Lewis Jersey, Bruce Jersey, Frank Decerbo, Al Mathewson, Jean Santopatre, Ventulett family, Ford Macieski, John Kochiss, Morgan Kaolian, Sarge Shaw, Alex Szabo, Ralph Harvey, Brad Williams, Rob Burlinson, Donald Bell, Jan Williams, Mike Forte, Gary Noren, Charles Dowd, Jean Baker, Faith Louvender, Mike Bielawa, and Hilliard Bloom.

We would also like to give our thanks to all of the photographers whose work was used in this book. Many of them were not identified on the old photographs and negatives. Without their images, however, there would be very few views of the late 19th and early 20th centuries.

INTRODUCTION

Bridgeport, a New England coastal city, often does not know it is a coastal city. Emphasis is placed on Interstate 95, speeding in and out of the city, to and from New York, or on Route 8, heading north to the suburbs.

Yet Bridgeport is indeed a New England coastal city, with a history as such. Glimmers of this history can be found in the Historical Collections Department at the Bridgeport Public Library, back in shelves in the library stacks. Old volumes labeled "U.S. Customs House, License of Vessels," dated as early as 1797, show ship after ship going out of Bridgeport, carrying cargo from exotic places like the West Indies, captained by local names such as Capt. John Brooks or Captain Burroughs.

Street names in Bridgeport also give a clue that there existed a nautical past. Atlantic Street, Seaview Avenue, Seabright Avenue, and Anchorage Drive all give a coastal flair to this area near the Sound. Old organizations such as the Seaside Club, the Seaside Outing Club, or the Seaside Institute all used the coast for their identity. Remnants of a sea life can be found in the piles of oyster shells at the foot of Pembroke Street, another clue that the ocean really does exist somewhere out there.

Our Bridgeport ancestors used Long Island Sound for their livelihood. They used it for fishing and for transporting goods. Many residents chose (and still choose) to live near the water; residents such as P.T. Barnum placed his house facing the Sound, so the fine Long Island shore breezes helped soothe the heat of inland life.

Bruce Williams, his father (Kaye), and his family never stopped using Long Island Sound. They continued to live in a community that managed, even today, to make a living from the Sound. Their heritage of working lobster boats, running a marina, and enjoying Sound life has helped immensely in forming this book.

Bruce and I have gathered here a view of what life near Long Island Sound was like for our Bridgeport ancestors. They lived, worked, and played by the Sound, making it a part of their lives. We hope this book will help reclaim the lost heritage of Long Island Sound and bring it into the 21st century.

—Mary K. Witkowski
Head, Historical Collections
Bridgeport Public Library

George Burroughs Torrey was a Bridgeport artist who painted portraits of businessmen, dignitaries, and U.S. presidents. His paintings of local seascapes, however, are among his best works. This painting, entitled *At the Wheel,* shows friends of Torrey doing what they loved—sailing on Long Island Sound. Torrey was born in 1863, living on Fairfield Avenue. He was related to Capt. Isaac Burroughs, whose fortune helped to finance the Bridgeport Public Library. Torrey's widow gave this painting, as well as several others, to the Bridgeport Public Library in 1942. Another large seascape portrait of local oysterman Capt. Bill Lewis at the wheel of a boat can be viewed in the Bridgeport Public Library, along with several other Torrey paintings.

One

Harbor Views

The Upper Wharves on Black Rock Harbor, shown here in 1880, are where the customs house, chandleries, and shipyards of the old port were located. With its deep and protected channel, Black Rock had risen in prominence as a seaport in the late 1700s. During the Revolutionary War, privateers sailed for its wharves to harass British shipping. While under the cover of darkness, whaleboats left to raid the Tory towns on the North Shore of Long Island. After an economic downturn brought on by the embargo of 1808 and War of 1812, the port once again began to flourish. It became a major shipbuilding center in the period from 1845 to 1865. As the steamboat era emerged after the Civil War, however, fortunes declined along the Black Rock waterfront. Not as dependent on wind and a deep channel as sailing vessels were, steamers could easily navigate the wind-locked, shallower Bridgeport Harbor with its attractive railroad connections to the north. Black Rock soon became a backwater port; its famous shipyards were relegated to repair and outfitting work.

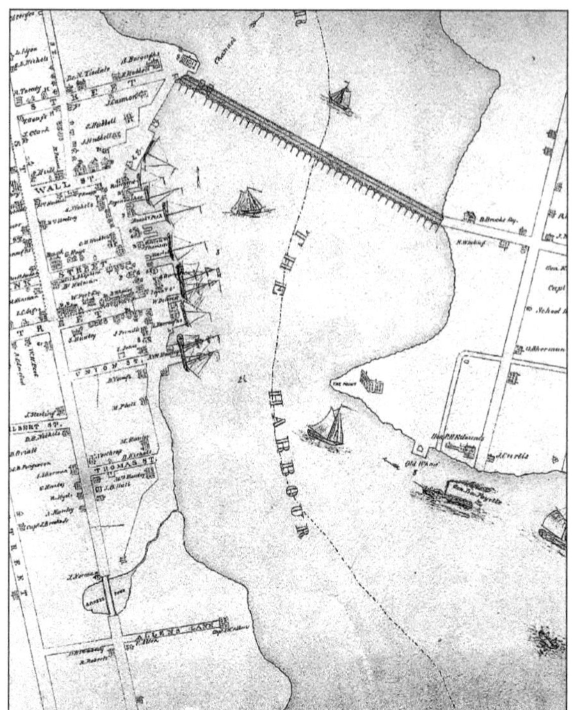

This 1824 hand-drawn map shows details of the Bridgeport Harbor area. Numerous wharves line Water Street, and drawings of ships highlight the captains that sailed out of the harbor to the West Indies and exotic ports of call. Fayerweather, Burroughs, Hawley, and DeForest are some of the names of early shipping merchants.

An 1875 panoramic view of Bridgeport shows incredible details of buildings, ships, and bridges. This close-up of the map shows the railroad dock (left) and roundhouse with the steamer *Bridgeport* leaving the harbor. Moving freight from water to rail to northern areas of Connecticut made Bridgeport a desirable harbor.

An old tide mill that was built on a pond in the city's East Side gave the waterway its name, which is now Yellow Mill Pond. The tide mill was built by Joseph Walker in 1792. Later owned by George Cook, the mill itself was destroyed by fire in 1884. The mill was at that time called Cook's Mill.

Shown here is a view looking north on Water Street *c.* 1890. The David Trubee and Company warehouses can be seen on the lower left. Beyond the Stratford Avenue Bridge are the Wheeler and Howes Coal Company and the Frank Miller Lumber Yard. Currently, the Water Street area is the site of the new passenger terminal for the Bridgeport and Port Jefferson Steamboat Company ferries. The terminal also serves as the headquarters for the Bridgeport Port Authority and Harbormaster's Department.

The ice-choked Bridgeport Harbor is seen in a view looking south on a cold winter's day in 1893. Coal barges await discharge on Water Street while, at the center left, a channel cuts through to the oyster houses at the foot of East Main Street. During abnormally cold winters, ice presents a serious impediment to navigation on both Bridgeport and Black Rock Harbors. Early local journals reported that during a period of severe winters in the late 18th and early 19th centuries, the harbors were often frozen and rendered impassable. The last major freeze in the area was over the winter of 1977–78, when ice measured up to 15 inches thick on Black Rock Harbor.

In 1888, the Bridgeport Grain Elevator (left) towers over the harbor in the western view across the Bridgeport Harbor. Several vessels lie along the Water Street side, including a lighter, oyster steamer and the steamer *Rosedale* (far upper right) at its pier just south of the Stratford Avenue Bridge. In the foreground a gentleman sculls a sharpie, a type of vessel developed in New Haven for both oystering and pleasure use.

Water Street is seen here in a view looking north on the Bridgeport Harbor c. 1890. In the foreground are a three-masted schooner and a canal barge unloading cargo. Just above them, the cross-sound ferry departs. Beyond the ferry, trolleys and horse-drawn wagons cross the Stratford Avenue Bridge, built in 1888.

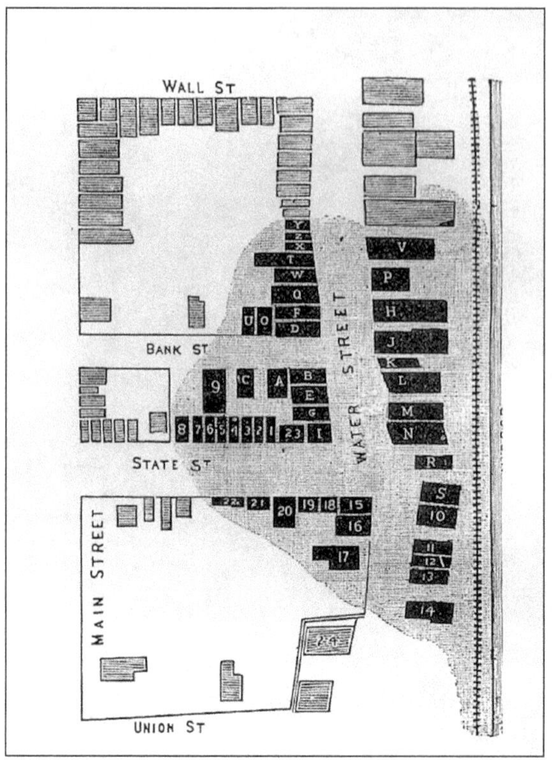

On December 16, 1845, George Wells woke up to find his oyster saloon and boardinghouse on Bank Street downtown in flames. Wells and his family escaped as firefighters arrived. The wind was coming from the northwest and spread quickly throughout the Water Street area. The tide was low, the weather was extremely cold, and the firemen had trouble pumping water from the Sound to put out the quickly moving flames. There were 49 buildings, mostly wooden, that were destroyed by the fire. Because there were several boardinghouses in the area, several families were displaced by the fire.

Water Street is shown in an 1888 view looking south. The Bridgeport Grain Elevator provided an excellent vantage point for a bird's-eye view of the harbor. The busy Naugatuck Railroad dock lies below on the left. Off in the distance, near the harbor entrance, is the South End site, where today lies the new Bluefish Stadium and the Sound Tigers hockey arena.

Oyster houses are seen in this view at the foot of Pembroke Street on the city's East Side, 1896. Out in the harbor, sloops return from a day of oystering on the Sound.

Shown here is an 1890s view from the Stratford Avenue Bridge. To the left is the dock of the Old Mohawk Yacht Club, once located on the south side of the bridge. In the center of the photograph is the oyster boat anchorage known as the "pen."

This is a view from the corner of Housatonic Avenue and Hall Street in 1896. On the left are the Aluminum, Brass and Bronze Company, the Housatonic Ice Company, and the old gashouse. This area is just west of the Pequonnock River.

Bridgeport Harbor teems with activity in this 1888 view. In the foreground is the menhaden fleet. These vessels pursued the large schools of menhaden (locally known as bunker fish), which migrated to the Sound during the summer months. This fishery is still active on the East Coast, and "bunker boats" can still be seen off the coast of Bridgeport. In the upper right, the steamer *Waterbury* backs into the Bridgeport Steamboat Company wharf. The *Waterbury* carried passengers between Bridgeport and New York from 1872 to 1891. Anchored around the periphery of the harbor are numerous small oyster sloops, part of a fleet of some 300 sloops that worked the Bridgeport oyster beds.

In 1919, from the open cockpit of a small biplane, Brewer H. Sholund took a series of remarkable photographs of the Bridgeport and Stratford coastline. This view shows Black Rock Harbor. The huge landfill that now bridges the area between Seaside Park and Fayerweather Island does not yet exist, but a causeway has been built from the park out to the island. The dark narrow line in the center of the photograph is one of two stone breakwaters constructed in the mid-19th century to protect the inner harbor. Off to the right, most of the old warehouses of the upper wharves, built in the glory days of the port, still stand.

In this Brewer H. Sholund view of Seaside Park, the beautiful homes lining the park, the Perry Memorial Arch, baseball diamonds, and the athletic track are clearly visible. The Locomobile plant can be seen just to the upper left of the park.

This Sholund photograph shows the Lake Torpedo Boat Company yards at the foot of Seaview Avenue. Prior to World War I, the Lake Torpedo Boat Company was able to produce only five submarines per year. Spurred on by wartime orders after 1914, new water lots were acquired on adjoining Johnson's Creek, which quadrupled the plant's capacity. Alongside the Lake Torpedo Boat Company yard, construction is under way on a bridge out to Pleasure Beach. The area along Seaview Avenue between Buckley Brothers and what used to be Parsell's Marina, now Dolphin's Cove, is still a thriving area for fishermen today. You can watch fishermen bring in their catches, often big crates of lobster, as you sit on the deck of Dolphin's Cove.

Seen here is an aerial view looking north on the Pequonnock River in 1978. On the center left is the old railroad station built in 1904–05. A year after this photograph was taken, the station burned to the ground. The *Miss New York*, a former Staten Island ferry, lies by its berth on the river. After undergoing a major restoration, the ferry was operated as a restaurant for several years. Just across the river is the Bridgeport Jai-Alai fronton, which opened in 1976.

It seems as if the red and white structure that towers over Bridgeport Harbor has always been part of the city's identity. The 500-foot smokestack, however, was built in 1967 by United Illuminating, at that time the highest smokestack of any Connecticut generating plant. The striped smokestack has become a landmark on the Sound.

Two

Living on the Sound

In 1788, Capt. John Brooks Sr. built this house on Pembroke Street in an area in East Bridgeport called New Pasture Point. The house was built for Brooks after he got married to Mary Coe in 1787. Descendants of the Brooks family lived in the house until it was finally willed to the Discovery Museum. The house was moved to the museum grounds near Ninety Acres Park, where it remains today.

Capt. John Brooks Jr. was born in East Bridgeport in the area known as New Pasture Point. Following in the footsteps of his father, Brooks captained a sloop at the age of 18 and later commanded steamboats most of his life. It was through the efforts of John Brooks Jr., who served as city alderman and twice as mayor of Bridgeport, that the harbor of Bridgeport was finally deepened. Brooks also worked to obtain a lighthouse for the city.

I will try to make the Best of it — The Last of my Corn
is full of Weavels 280 Bushel of it I have sold @ 6/ this Currancy
to hear No more of it. But if any Objection should be made, Respecting
it I shall be Obliged to make an Abatement — the Sale of the Cargo
in Guardilupa the Cattle @ 5 Joes, the horses @ 4½ Joes... Part of the
[illegible] ℔ Barr, Part of the Beef from 9½ to 9 dollars ℔ Barr, here I have
as Above mentioned & have sold the hoops @ 3 Joes ℔ m Staves @ 2½ Joes
& am Retailing the Remainder of the Beef @ 10 & 9 dollars ℔ Barr —
so Late and produce the Object of the Voyage it will detain me Longer
Perhaps all March — shall however do all in my Power to despatch
[illegible], we are all well on board; and I mentioned in my former Letter I
alive & in Midling Order — if you think of a Summer Voyage let me
to provide in Season. Marketts are so Precarious its in Vain to Mention

I am with due Respect

Bishop of New Haven — your most humb Servt

Shown is a 1788 letter from Capt. John Brooks Sr. to Hubbell regarding the sale of corn and other goods. Brooks was in the West Indies at the time.

This old shipbuilder's shop at the foot of East Main Street was owned by Charles H. Morris. Before it was used for building ships, however, the house was used as a smugglers' cove, even before the Revolution. Boats were said to have slipped along the wharf and load and unload secret cargo from this site. This photograph was from a glass-plate negative taken *c.* 1908.

During the War of 1812, Capt. Joel Thorp commanded the sloop *Othello*, which was captured by the British. This house on Lafayette Street is thought to have been built by Captain Thorp. Dating of the home varied between 1800 to 1835. Dr. Willard and Ella Fleck owned the house in later years. The house eventually became a restaurant known as Hitching Post Inn and was torn down in the 1960s.

Catherine Burroughs Pettengill, daughter of Capt. Isaac Burroughs, inherited a fortune from her father's shipping empire. Upon her death in 1881, Catherine Pettengill bequeathed the Burroughs Building at the corner of Main and John Streets to the Bridgeport Public Library for a permanent home. For many years, stores were located in the first floor while the library resided in the upper floors of the building. Still carrying the Burroughs name, the Bridgeport Public Library built a new building at the corner of State and Broad Streets in 1927.

Jurgan Frederick Huge (1809–1878) was a German immigrant who painted many local scenes, including this watercolor of the Burroughs Building, 1876. This painting, along with several others, are owned by the Bridgeport Public Library, including a painting of the Bridgeport lightboat. A painting of Capt. John Brooks Jr.'s steamboat the *Nimrod* by Huge is at the Barnum Museum.

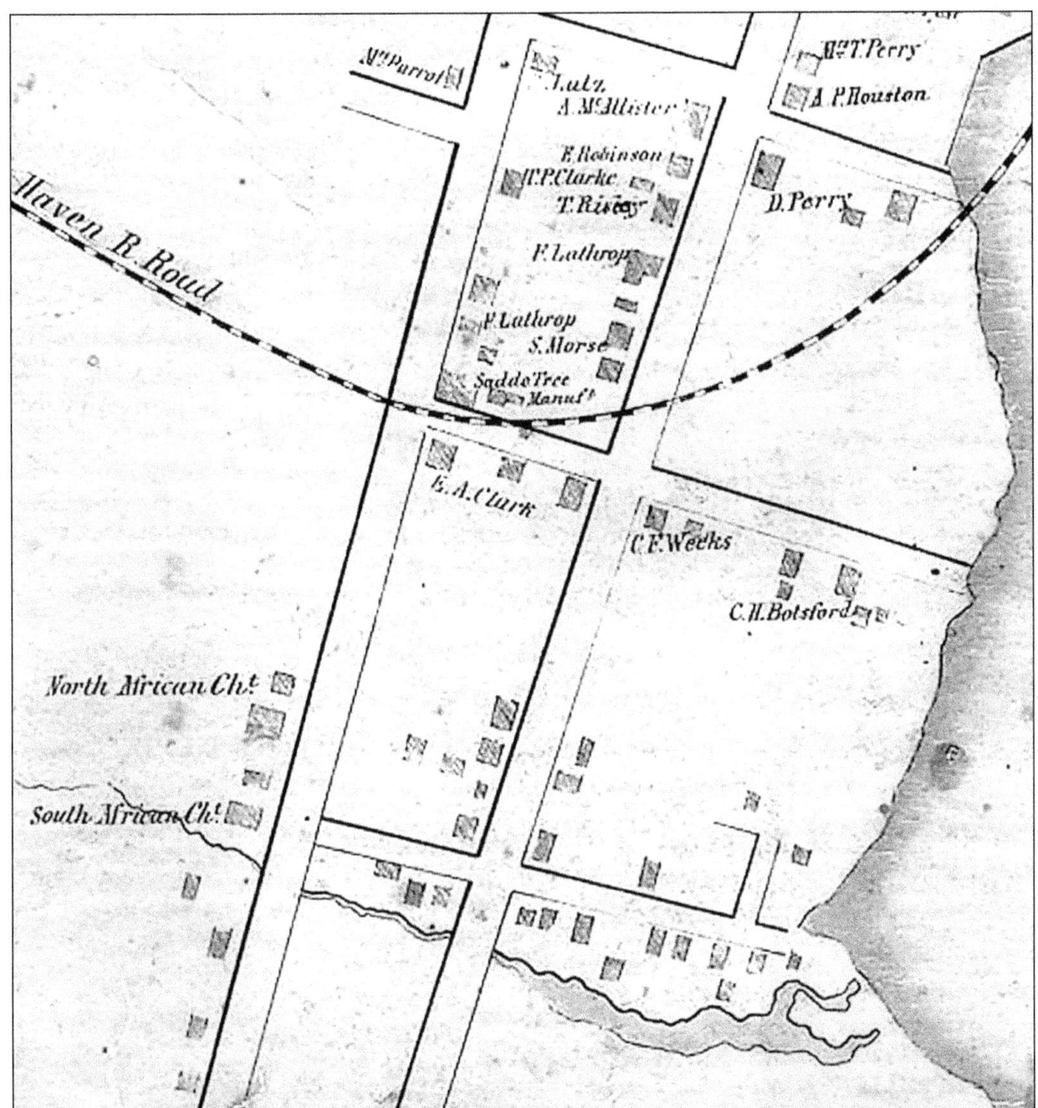

This 1850 map of Bridgeport shows two churches on Broad Street in the city's South End, just a couple of blocks from the harbor, designated as North African Church and South African Church. Many black residents lived in the area around the churches, an area sometimes called "Little Liberia." Across the street from the churches, the second and third houses in from the corner of Main and Whiting Streets going north are the two houses that were owned by Eliza and Mary Freeman, built by the sisters in 1848. These houses are on the National Register of Historic Places and are considered the oldest existing houses in the city built and owned by African Americans.

The African Methodist Church in the city was formed by members of the black community in 1826 on the site of the present Bridgeport Public Library. In 1835, a church was built by the African Methodist congregation on Broad Street in the city's South End. In 1843, a split in ideology formed two churches: the AME Zion Church and the Bethel AME Church. The Bethel AME Church is shown here at the corner of Broad and Whiting Streets.

AME Zion Church (now called Walter's Memorial AME Zion) laid its cornerstone on July 5, 1835, at the corner of Broad and Gregory Streets. While originally part of the larger AME congregation started in 1826, the congregation started its own church at this location, where it can still be found today.

Members of the AME Zion Church pose on the front steps of the church in a photograph taken around the beginning of the 20th century. P.T. Barnum gave some financial support to the church when this edifice was built in 1882. This photograph, made from a glass-plate negative was recently discovered, and identifications have not yet been made. Anyone knowing the names of the church members pictured here should please contact the authors.

A horsecar journeys down Main Street after dropping off a woman near Kiefer Street in the Little Liberia section. Tracks continued down to Seaside Park and the foot of Main Street. This 1892 view was taken on a snowy day—notice the woman bundled for winter weather.

Page No. 287

SCHEDULE 1.—Free Inhabitants in Bridgeport **in the Co**

of Conn **enumerated by me, on the** 30th **day of** July **1860**

Post Office Bridgeport

Dwelling-houses—numbered in the order of visitation.	Families numbered in the order of visitation.	The name of every person whose usual place of abode on the first day of June, 1860, was in this family.	Description. Age.	Sex.	Color, {White, black, or mulatto.	Profession, Occupation, or Trade of each person, male and female, over 15 years of age.	Value of Estate Owned. Value of Real Estate.	Value of Personal Estate.
979	2239	Burr Knapp	63	M		Sea Captain	50,000	50,000
979	2239	Marietta Knapp	58	F				
		Marietta	19	F				

Capt. Burr Knapp, who was the skipper of the schooner *Moonlight*, kept a journal of one of his trips along the coast from New Jersey to Alabama and along the Potomac. He joined with P.T. Barnum to give land to build Seaside Park. Here is his listing in the 1860 federal census. His occupation is listed as sea captain. His value of real estate is listed as $50,000 and his personal estate is listed as $50,000, a large sum of money in that day. The journal is housed in the Historical Collections Department of the Bridgeport Public Library.

The Hezekiah Osborn house, built in 1801, was located at the foot of Brewster Street by the Upper Wharves. For many years it was the home of Charles H. Fancher, merchant, lobsterman, and one-time Bridgeport harbormaster. From his wharf behind the house, Fancher ran a successful lobster and fish business for many years. In this 1910 photograph, the three-story Thompson and Fancher warehouse can be seen just beyond the house.

Edwards Johnson, grandson of William S. Johnson (signer of the Constitution), built the house he called Eagle's Nest in 1830. The house was surrounded by 300 acres, and oysters were plentiful in the nearby creek (later called Johnson's Creek). In 1844, Johnson sold the house to Joseph de Rivera, a sugar and wine merchant from Puerto Rico. The Rivera family lived in the house until 1858, when they moved to Ohio to start a vineyard. The house is still on 282–284 Logan Street.

Once called "Bridgeport's oldest living resident," the Johnson Oak stood majestically near the corner of Logan and Alex Streets in the city's East End, a living monument for more than 500 years. Named after the owner of the property, the tree was more than 100 feet high. In 1978, early one sunny Sunday morning, the tree split as the result of the rotting inside its trunk. The Johnson Oak Tree Park is still on the city's East End.

In the 1880s, the Dundon brothers, Richard and Thomas, established a coal yard at the head of Burr Creek, a branch of Black Rock Harbor once navigable up to Fairfield Avenue. In 1893, Richard Dundon built a Queen Anne–style home (shown in 1921) alongside the coal yard. In 1902, the house was purchased by the Koletar family, who occupied it for the next 50 years. The Dundon house was moved in 1991 to its present location on Black Rock Harbor, where it now serves as a museum highlighting Bridgeport's rich maritime heritage.

The Edward Dennis house was built in 1852 on Maiden Lane in the city's New Pasture Point area. It was constructed in early Victorian Vernacular style and remained in the Dennis family for over 107 years. The recently demolished Dennis house stood in the heart of one of Bridgeport's most vibrant waterfront districts, a center of fishing and shipbuilding.

The old powerhouse channel cuts through the Cilco terminal property on Seaview Avenue. In the late 19th century, its banks were lined with squatters' cabins, shown here *c.* 1895.

The New Pasture Point area is shown looking down California Street, with Pembroke Street in the foreground. This is the site of some of Bridgeport's earliest waterfront activity. The area of pilings on the upper right near the water is the former site of the cross-sound ferry landing. It is now the site of MOVE Yacht Club. This area has been cleared for potential harbor development.

In 1848, P.T. Barnum built his "oriental villa" on grounds just north of what is Seaside Park (around what are now Iranistan and Fairfield Avenues).
P.T. Barnum was known for his extravagant parties at the impressive mansion and, at that time, the grounds were still countryside. The mansion grounds were beautifully landscaped and the house was a strange mixture of Moorish and other Eastern influences. Barnum used an engraving of his house on his letterhead, shown here in a note written *c.* 1849 inviting friends to visit. The house was destroyed by fire in 1857. Citizens of Bridgeport ran down to the scene of the fire to help save some of the furniture, which is now on display at the Barnum Museum.

P.T. Barnum built his third home, Waldemere, closer to Seaside Park in 1868–69, overlooking the water. The name Waldemere meant "woods by the sea" and showed Barnum's fondness for Long Island Sound. He wanted his wife, Charity (who was often ailing), to be refreshed and invigorated by the sea air. Barnum's daughter Caroline actually lived in one of the cottages on the grounds with her family. Visitors such as Mark Twain and Horace Greeley would often stop by the house.

This porch view of Waldemere, taken in 1875, shows the ornate Victorian design of the house's columns. Carriages were able to drive right up to the front door to pick up P.T. Barnum and his family and continue on the long, winding driveway.

As is evident in this view from the porch of Waldemere, the grounds surrounding the house were vast, with ornate fountains and sculptures throughout the area. In 1875, when this photograph was taken, P.T. Barnum served a one-year term as mayor of Bridgeport. When Mayor Barnum was home from his many travels, a flag was raised above the house.

This engraving from an 1875 map of Bridgeport shows P.T. Barnum's house Waldemere with its spectacular view of Long Island Sound with sailboats in the distance. Shown also are the ornate grounds with fountains.

P.T. Barnum lived in Waldemere with his family for 20 years, enjoying the house that became cluttered with many treasures from his travels. Charity Barnum died in November 1873, when Barnum was traveling in Europe. While in England, P.T. Barnum secretly married a young English woman, Nancy Fish, on February 14, 1874. Barnum returned to the United States after the marriage, keeping his marriage to Fish a secret. In September 1874, Barnum married her in a civil marriage in New York, bringing her home to Waldemere to live. In 1888, Barnum began building a new home for his young bride, a less drafty home with electric lighting and good plumbing. The new brick house was built right next to the old house. The house was named Marina, once again showing Barnum's love of the sea. When Waldemere was dismantled, part of it was moved to 624 Atlantic Street and the other to 1 Pauline Street in Lordship, where they are still located.

Bridgeport Public Works Department set aside the morning of December 8, 1888, to test the newly built Stratford Avenue Bridge. Helping to test the bridge were more than 200 Bridgeport citizens along with P.T. Barnum and 12 of his circus elephants. P.T. Barnum is the white-haired man in the center standing in front of his elephants. Good news—the bridge did not collapse!

Electric trolley cars were first used in Bridgeport in 1894 and, by 1906, trolley lines ran throughout the city. Trolleys could take you to your favorite destination, be it Newfield Park to play baseball, or Seaside Park to take a swim, as this Main Street trolley's signs showed. In the winter, problems arose when the tracks became covered with drifts, making it difficult for trolleys to continue their routes. When cars and buses became a more familiar mode of transit, many of the trolley lines were shut down. The East Main Street and North Main Street trolleys were the last to run in Bridgeport, taking their final trip in 1937. Removal of trolley tracks began with the state coordinating efforts between the city and WPA workers in the 1930s.

Pedestrians walking near the railroad station prior to 1902 had to walk quickly to dodge the incoming trains as they came into the station. Train tracks were level with the street, so elevating the tracks became a matter of safety for local residents. Many a politician, including P.T. Barnum himself, campaigned to elevate the train tracks.

This *c.* 1897 photograph shows the beginning of work being done to elevate the tracks, so that no more accidents would occur. Wood and stone is piled high, ready to be used in construction. The Atlantic Hotel is visible behind the train station.

Students of the old Prospect School and their teacher, Miss Blansfield, pose for a photograph in 1888 on the steps of their school in the city's South End. Jasper McLevy is the grim-faced student in the front row, center. In 1960, Mayor Jasper McLevy attended the 100th anniversary of the school, which was the city's only public school at one time. The school was torn down in 1963.

Black Rock was a community with long ties to the sea. In 1819, in a village of approximately 100 inhabitants, it was reported that 28 men were gone as sailors, half of them captains. Pictured *c.* 1900 is the second Black Rock School. It was built in 1865 and stood near the intersection of Grovers Avenue and Brewster Street. It was replaced by the present Black Rock School on Brewster Street in 1905.

This view looks south on Black Rock Harbor from the foot of Beacon Street in 1912. On the upper right, just beyond the Bridgeport Yacht Club, is the Bartram estate. A number of yachts, both sail and power, are under way or lie at anchor at the harbor mouth.

The Anchorage, shown *c.* 1909, was built by financier Percy Bartram in 1904. The estate sits near the entrance to Black Rock Harbor on the site of the old Squire's Wharf. According to legend, the pirate Captain Kidd was thought to have buried treasure on the sandy shore near the house. To this day, the shoreline surrounding the house is known as "Money Beach."

Ladies pose for a group portrait in a Hackley Street backyard *c.* 1905. Just beyond them is Burr Creek, the west reach of Black Rock Harbor.

The picturesque St. Mary's by the Sea was located down on the shore at the western end of Grover's Hill. It was built in 1893 by Thomas Pearsall, whose estate is visible on the hill to the right. The chapel's beautiful altar, stained-glass windows, organ, and chimes attracted many affluent families for Sunday services. After Pearsall's death St. Mary's fell into disrepair until World War I, when the nearby U.S. Naval Reserve Corps began to use it for services.

Members of the Fancher and Noren families prepare to launch a model yacht on the waters of Black Rock Harbor *c.* 1910. The stone wall to the left fronts the property now occupied in the Fayerweather Towers condominiums. In the distance is one of the warehouses of the Upper Wharves, which is now the clubhouse of the Port 5 Naval Veterans Association.

They looked like the real thing, but they were really boat models that accurately copied full-rigged ships down to the rigging and sails. Local children would sail these model yachts in the pond in Seaside Park called Mirror Lake or in other shallow waters around the city. Children who built these sailing ships were members of a local club called Model Yacht Club and often met at the South End Library branch, pictured here. Black Rock and Newfield Library also had Model Yacht Clubs, and all the libraries had a special corner in which ships and nautical books were displayed. Here members of the Model Yacht Club pose before leaving the South End Library branch to race their models in Seaside Park.

This view shows lower Ellsworth Street in Black Rock *c.* 1900. On the right is the house of shipbuilder William Hall, built in 1856. The beautifully restored Hall house still stands today, one of the homes preserved within the Black Rock Historic District. To the left is the present site of Ellsworth Field, home of the Black Rock Little League.

An unidentified young lady stands at the corner of present-day Seaview Terrace and Seabright Avenue *c.* 1910. In the background are the office and warehouses of the Burr Coal Company on Black Rock Harbor. William Howes, a former captain of whaling vessels from Sag Harbor, Long Island, established the first coal business at this wharf.

Lewis F. Curtis was an inventor of note and president of People's Savings Bank. His house was built in 1910, when Curtis had an elegant Mediterranean-style palazzo designed by architect Ernest G. Southey. Curtis lived in the house until his death in 1938, when it was bequeathed to the Diocese of Bridgeport.

This view of the Curtis Mansion was taken during the Barnum Festival in 1962. The Curtis Mansion was torn down in 1987 when the Diocese of Bridgeport sold the property for condominiums that were never built. The lot is vacant except for the mansion's once tile-roofed garage.

After World War I, a summer colony developed on the northern end of Fayerweather Island. The first residents camped out in surplus tents, which were gradually replaced by more permanent cottages and cabins. This 1930s photograph shows the colony and a number of small pleasure craft on Black Rock Harbor.

Charlie Dowd and Charles Hawman spar by Black Rock Harbor in 1918. The match takes place on the beach, which ran between the old Middle Wharf and the SS Norden Swedish Singing Society Club at the foot of Beacon Street. The Norden Club is still active today and can be seen behind the boys.

When the Newfield Branch Library opened its doors in 1922, it soon became the city's most popular branch. Located only a couple of blocks from the Sound, the branch had a Marine Club, which had weekly story hours for the children where tales of the sea, sailors, and pirates were told. Here, children sit on the steps of Newfield Branch Library in 1922.

Vivian Laborde leans against her dory on Fayerweather Island in 1937. Behind Laborde is one of the small cottages of the popular island community. The center of activity on the island was Bloomer's, which provided boat rentals, bait, and groceries to the residents. A number of cottages were destroyed or damaged in the Hurricane of 1938. The rest were torn down by the city in 1944, putting an end to one of Bridgeport's most colorful coastal neighborhoods.

During World War I, every area of Bridgeport's waterfront was scrutinized to make sure it was well protected. Here city officials, along with Mayor Wilson (center) inspect the Stratford Avenue Bridge.

In April 1921, in a basement on Main Street, the New Era Lodge was formed as part of the Order of Elks. Membership in the club grew quickly, from 6 original members to 200. An annual ball, shown here in 1923, was one of the highlights of the club's activities. The lodge has always been active in the community, helping to fund new housing and special projects. The New Era Lodge is now located at 560 Newfield Avenue in the city's East End, celebrating its 80th anniversary.

The Plaza, an area near Water and State Streets, was the center of wholesale trade as well as traffic in downtown Bridgeport. Garden trucks came at dawn until nearly high noon, and the plaza was described in one newspaper article as "resembling the public market square of a prosperous European town, only less orderly and tidy." Remnants of the older buildings from the glory days of Bridgeport's seafaring days, such as boardinghouses and taverns, were scattered in the area, some of the earliest buildings in Bridgeport. It was said that at night, trucks would come in and illegally bring in alcohol. Older lodging houses and former saloons were used as speakeasies.

The James Van Dyke Company at the corner of Main and John Streets was known for its imported coffee and teas from all over the world, as well as other imported goods. Immigrants to the city who had a special hankering for the brew from the old country could find it on the shelves of Van Dyke's. Across the street was the P & Q shop, one of the early discount stores in the city.

The site of the old Eastern Malleable Iron Company was the choice for the new South End federal housing project. At the groundbreaking for the project on August 31, 1940, Mayor Jasper McLevy spoke to a crowd gathered at South and Iranistan Avenues. The Reverend Stephen J. Panik, chairman of the Bridgeport Housing Authority, also spoke to the crowd. The first residents of the project, named Marina in a contest after P.T. Barnum's last home, moved into the housing in February 1941.

Rationing of many products during World War II, such as food items, gasoline, and coffee, caused a surge in the black market—products were sold secretly to the highest bidder. In August 1943, a rally in Marina Park was held to protest the black market. Shown attending the rally are, from left to right, the following: (front row) Franz Rupp, pianist; Marian Anderson, opera singer; Bud Hulick, comedian; Carl Frank, radio announcer and actor; (back row) Franklin P. Adams, columnist and quiz expert; Mayor Jasper McLevy; Edna Ferber, novelist; and Clifton Fadiman, book reviewer for the *New Yorker*.

In 1931, the Junior Garden Club met at the South Branch Library, holding an annual September flower show. More than 100 gardens were planted throughout the city, and the children learned about herbs, such as St. John's Wort and Yarrow. The Junior Garden Club was featured in national magazines. Located in an industrial neighborhood right by the harbor, the gardens were varied and abundant. Note the smokestacks of the Bassick Company to the library's right.

The Hurricane of 1938 caused considerable damage throughout the city, destroying many trees, particularly in Seaside Park and the surrounding South End. In this photograph, residents of Atlantic Street survey the uprooted tree in front of their houses. These houses were built in 1877 and designed by the Palliser Brothers, Bridgeport architects who sold their mail-order house plans throughout the United States.

Built to house the growing population of Bridgeport workers during World War I, this carefully planned development was one of the finest of several housing projects built in the city. The Bridgeport Housing Company developed planned neighborhoods like Seaside Village, with courtyards and small backyards, carefully laid out for families to own their own homes in privacy. This photograph was taken in 1963, showing the well-cared-for and shady streets.

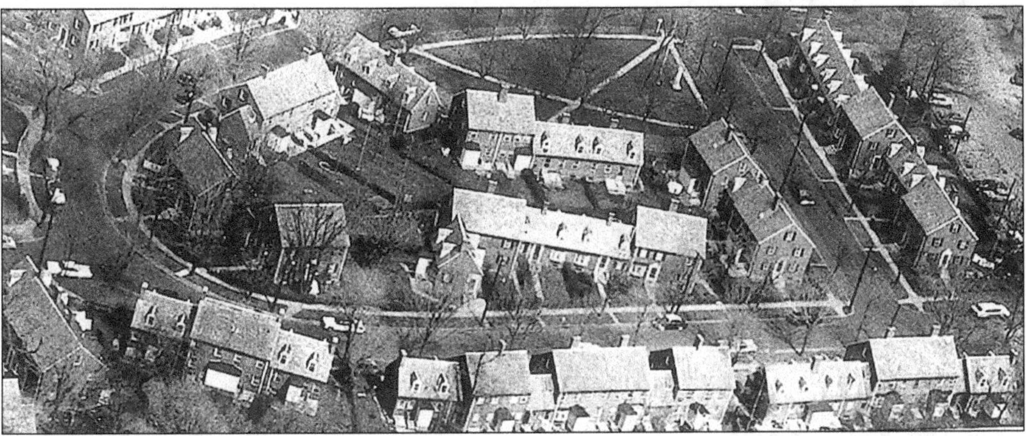
This aerial view of Seaside Village shows the symmetry of the streets. Located just a stone's throw from Seaside Park, the housing development is as attractive now as it was 80 years ago, when it was built.

On October 8, 1936, as a tribute to Bridgeport's centennial, more than 150,000 people watched the *Hindenburg* as it circled twice around the Park City. From the East End to Black Rock, cheering people stood on rooftops of houses and factory buildings. Mayor Jasper McLevy sent a radiogram to the commander of the *Hindenburg*, Dr. Hugo Eckener. On May 6, 1937, the airship burned while docking at Lakehurst, New Jersey. Thirty-five passengers died, including the captain, Ernst Lehmann.

Three

MAKING A LIVING ON THE SOUND

The *Sarah Jane* was typical of the vessels launched by the shipyards of Black Rock in the pre–Civil War period. The best known of the Black Rock shipbuilders was William Hall, who operated four yards at the Upper Wharves. Hall launched the medium clipper *Charles Cooper* in 1856. At 165 feet and 900 tons, it was one of the largest vessels built in Black Rock. In 1866, while attempting to round Cape Horn, the *Charles Cooper* was damaged and driven back to Port Stanley in the Falkland Islands. It was pulled ashore in Port Stanley harbor, and its hull was covered by a corrugated tin roof to protect it from the elements. Still intact after nearly 150 years, it remains the only American-built packet in existence.

This harbor view was drawn by John Warner Barber in 1837. Several whaling companies were formed in the city in the 1830s. The largest was the Bridgeport Whaling Company, organized in 1833. The firm owned four boats: the *Atlantic*, the *Hamilton*, the *Harvest*, and the *Stieglitz*. One of the most successful voyages was the 1837–38 cruise of the *Atlantic*, when the ship harpooned 34 whales in the Atlantic and Indian Oceans. The whale ships generally landed along Water Street at the docks later operated by the Housatonic Railroad Company. The arrivals of these vessels were the cause of great excitement, especially among the relations and friends of long-absent crewmen. The 1826 house of David Perry, a financial backer of local whaling voyages, still stands at 531 Lafayette Street.

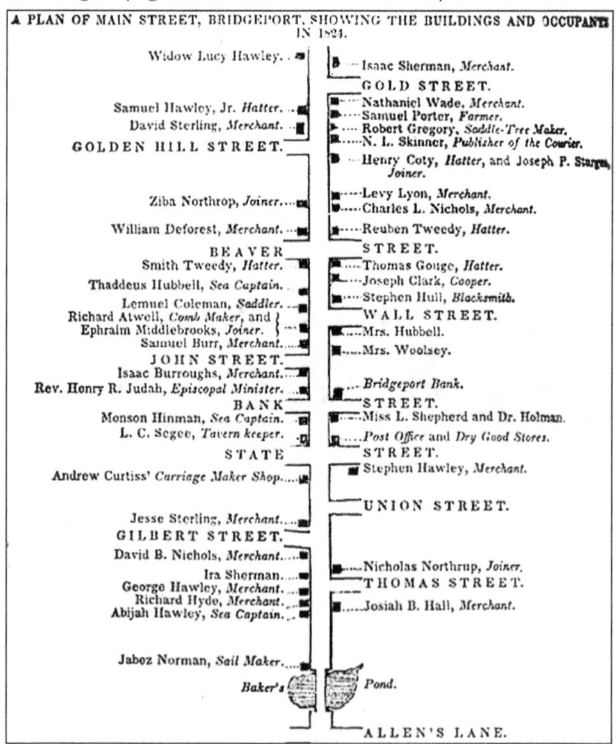

Shown on this map as it appeared in 1824, Main Street had the elements that were needed for a growing town. Merchants like Josiah B. Hall, a doctor, the Bridgeport Bank, plenty of hatters, saddlers, carpenters (joiners), and a carriage-maker shop lined Main Street. Also evident are the sea captains living on the street: Abijah Hawley, Monson Hinman, Thaddeus Hubbell, and sail maker Jabez Norman.

The *Perry Setzer* is seen here under construction at the Greene Brothers Shipyard in 1902. At 240 feet, it was the largest vessel built in the area since the medium clippers launched in the 1850s by the William Hall yard in Black Rock. The Greene Brothers, who hailed from Maine, built three other large schooners—the *P.T. Barnum*, *Sylvia C. Hall*, and *Greenleaf Johnson*.

A festive crowd attends the launching of the four-masted schooner *Perry Setzer* at the Greene Brothers shipyard in 1903. Moments after this photograph was taken, the ways beneath the vessel gave out. Greene Brothers built several other large schooners and a number of powered oyster boats, including the *Climax*, seen here on the lower left.

Tow lines from tugs operated by the Merritt, Chapman, and Scott Company attempt to pull the schooner *Perry Setzer* off damaged ways at the Greene Brothers shipyard on Seaview Avenue. Although being stuck on the ways at launching was considered a bad omen for a vessel, the *Setzer* had a relatively long career. Primarily engaged in the coaling trade, it worked steadily until lost on a shoal off North Carolina in 1924.

Since the first vessel was launched at the head of the Pequonnock River *c.* 1730, boatbuilding has been an important trade on Bridgeport Harbor. Here a crew poses before a small vessel being "planked up" at an unidentified boatyard near Pembroke Street, in the city's New Pasture Point section on the East Side *c.* 1910.

Shown in this view is Edward Speer's boatyard on Johnson's Creek. Speer was one of the last of the wooden boat builders in Bridgeport. Here the oyster sloop *Priscilla* sits in the yard awaiting repairs. The *Priscilla*, built on Long Island's South Shore in 1888, is one of a handful of sloops surviving from Bridgeport's once great oyster fleet. It is now restored and on display at the Long Island Maritime Museum in West Sayville, New York.

The *Anna R. Heidritter* is seen in this view at the West End Lumber Company yard wharf. By the 1930s, there was only a handful of schooners like the *Heidritter* still plying their trade along the coast. They survived by carrying bulk cargoes such as lath, logwood, southern pine, and coal. The *Heidritter,* built in 1903, was lost at sea in 1942.

Shown in this view are vessels tied along the West End Lumber Company wharf *c.* 1930. The area is the West End of Bridgeport on Cedar Creek, the northernmost reach of Black Rock Harbor. The larger of these two schooners is the four-masted *Anna R. Heidritter.*

A three-masted schooner is seen in this *c.* 1912 view at the North Yard of the Frank Miller Lumber Company. This firm, one of several large lumberyards in the city, was located on East Washington Avenue by the Pequonnock River. Although by this time cargo was increasingly moved by steam tugs and barges, a considerable amount of goods still moved by sail. In 1916 alone, 6,834 sailing vessels cleared the port of Bridgeport.

After heavy rainfall on July 30, 1905, the Bunnell's Pond Dam at Beardsley Park burst. It was reported that 11.36 inches of rain fell in 16 hours. Casualties included several houses and the lumber schooner *Hope Haynes*. The schooner appears here with its bowsprit piercing the Congress Street Bridge.

Shown here is the steam tug *Robert McAllister* on the west side of Bridgeport Harbor, just south of the Naugatuck Railroad dock. In the distance is the Locomobile plant. The tug was owned by the McAllister Towing Company, which also operated passenger steamers on the Sound and the Hudson River. Today, in addition to its extensive towing operations, McAllister Brothers owns the Bridgeport and Port Jefferson Steamboat Company, which the firm purchased from Joseph Tooker in 1960.

The dredge boat *Empire State* is seen c. 1915 in Bridgeport Harbor. Major improvements to the harbor first took place in 1844, when the government dredged a channel through the sandbar at the harbor entrance. A stone breakwater was also constructed in that year to protect the harbor from storms coming off the Sound. Credit for these early improvements goes to harbormaster Abraham A. McNeil, whose son Capt. John McNeil continued the harbor development, constructing a new lighthouse and adding to the breakwater in 1871.

Bridgeport's own "Tugboat Annie," Ruth MacDonald Allen, stands by the wheelhouse of the tug that bears her name. This photograph appeared in the *Bridgeport Times Star* on July 19, 1940. A former newspaper reporter, Allen was the owner of the Bridgeport Towing Line, which operated two other tugs, the *Sam Gregory* and the *Easton*.

In May 1947, *Bridgeport Post* photographer Frank Decerbo took this photograph of the tug *Ruth MacDonald* sunk at the Bridgeport Towing Line Company wharf. Bridgeport Towing went out of business several months later, citing a reduced demand for tugs on the harbor.

Canal barges were sturdy working vessels developed originally for moving cargo on the Hudson River and Erie Canal. These colorful working craft, whose owners often lived aboard, were also a common sight on the Sound. No less than 1,160 canal barges cleared the port of Bridgeport in 1934. Pictured here aboard the barge *Stephen J. Horkay* in 1935 is the vessel's crew, Capt. James Kelsey and Mrs. and Mrs. James Lane.

The menhaden steamer *J.W. French* is seen here fishing off Bridgeport in July 1900. This photograph was taken by Edwin Holmes from the deck of the yacht *Privateer*. These vessels used a type of net called a purse seine to trap large schools of menhaden, known locally as mossbunker or bunker. The skiffs alongside the steamer, usually manned by African American crews, were used to set the net. Menhaden were processed both for fertilizer and for their oil, which was valuable as a base for paint. The height of the fishery was in the 1880s, when a fleet of some 600 vessels pursued the fish in the waters off Connecticut and Long Island.

In the 1890s, more than 300 sloops worked the productive oyster beds off the Bridgeport coast. These sloops ranged in size from 25 feet to 45 feet and had a carrying capacity of up to 600 bushels of oysters. Oysters were caught by means of one or more dredges, which "scraped" oysters into a net bag when towed along the bottom. Here, the *J.F. Penney* dredges off Bridgeport. It was owned by the Ventulett family from 1935 until it was destroyed by a gasoline explosion in 1949.

The oyster dredges *Mollie M*, *Ellen S*, and the *Fearless* are seen here tied up in Bridgeport Harbor c. 1910. The *Mollie M* and the *Ellen S* were typical of the steam- or gasoline-powered vessels built at the beginning of the 20th century to work on private beds in the Sound. A number of boats of this type and vintage are still active. The *Fearless* was built in Maine as a schooner and later converted to power.

Shown in this photograph are Bridgeport oystermen Henry Treat and "Skinny" Rowland aboard Rowland's 50-foot sloop *Nena A. Rowland*. The *Nena* was the largest of the Connecticut oyster sloops. Built in Norwalk in 1883, it was known as the "Queen of the Sound" and could pull up to 18 oyster dredges at one time.

This view shows the oyster sloop *Harp* being freed from the ice in the Bridgeport Harbor *c*. 1935. The well-known *Harp* was built in Rowayton in 1873.

New Haven or Fair Haven sharpies ranged in size from 25 to 40 feet in length. They were normally used to tong for oysters on the rivers and creeks leading into the Sound. This sharpie was photographed in an unidentified yard in 1912.

The schooner *Bora Queen* is shown hauled out on the Hitchcock Marine railway in 1948. To the right are shell piles on the Radel Oyster Company property. Tallmadge Brothers, the largest shellfish producers on the Sound, now occupies the former Radel site.

This model of the oyster steamer *Alice* was built by Captain Larraby in 1923. During retirement, sea captains often built highly detailed models of the well-loved vessels they had served aboard. The real *Alice*, built in 1906, was owned by the H.J. Lewis Oyster Company, located on Bridgeport Harbor at the foot of Pembroke Street. *Alice* was an enclosed-type oyster steamer with a full house running nearly its entire length.

By the 1950s, Connecticut's once productive oyster beds had been ravaged by storms, pollution, and predators, thus reducing the once proud oystering fleet to the handful of venerable sloops pictured here at Henry Street in Bridgeport. Due to careful husbandry and increasingly better water quality in Long Island Sound, the local oyster industry has rebounded in recent years, and once again Connecticut is one of the leading shellfish producers in the nation.

The *Bluepoints* is shown here hauled out on the marine railway of the Hitchcock Gas Engine Company. The 92-foot *Bluepoints* was one of the largest oyster vessels to work on the Sound. It was built at Essex, Massachusetts, in 1931 and was operated by the Connecticut Oyster Farms in Milford. Standing on the scaffold to the far left is Alex Szabo, master shipwright at the yard for many years.

Here, the crews of small wooden scows offload oysters onto the *George F. Carman*. The *Carman* is acting here as a "buy boat," purchasing juvenile, or seed oysters, off the scows. The oysters will be taken out to offshore beds next, where they will be grown to market size. When this *c.* 1950 photograph was taken, the captains of the scows received about 50¢ per bushel of oysters.

Elias Howe Jr. built his large sewing machine factory in 1863, right on the east side of the Pequonnock River. This idealized depiction of the Howe factory shows a glamorous view of the building and shoreline. However, Howe's building truly was a beautifully domed building and did have a fountain in front of it. Howe also had his own dock for direct shipping to and from New York. A fire in 1883 destroyed the main building.

Workers from the Crane Company on Main Street pose for a photograph in 1907. Among other products, Crane produced cast-iron fittings and brass works. Crane had taken over the old factory of Eaton, Cole and Burnham, later the site of Jenkins Brothers.

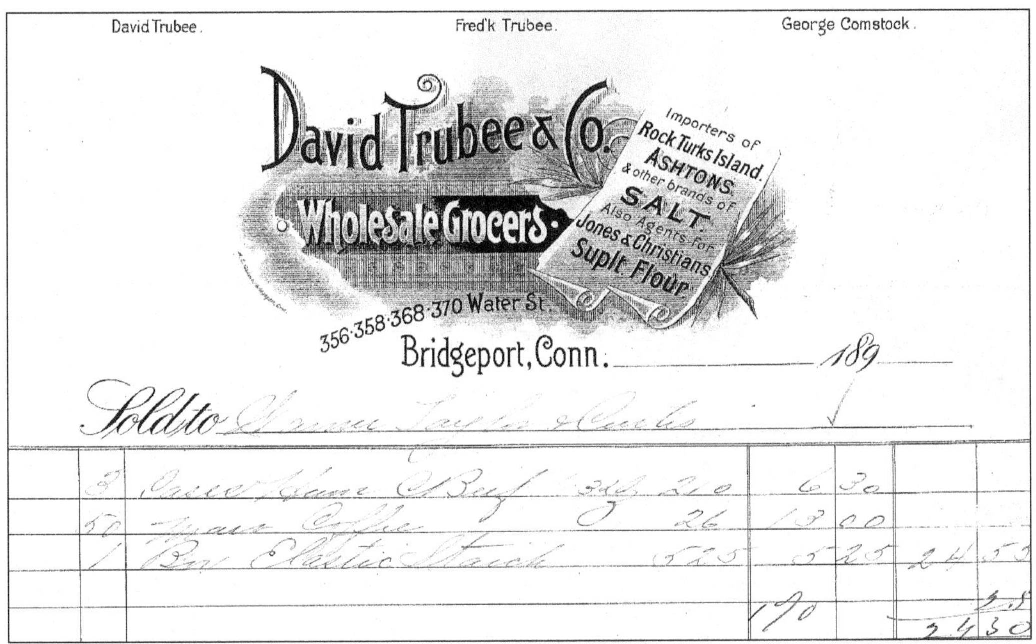

David Trubee. Fred'k Trubee. George Comstock.

David Trubee & Co.

Wholesale Grocers.

Importers of Rock Turks Island. Ashtons & other brands of Salt. Also Agents for Jones & Christians Suplt. Flour.

356·358·368·370 Water St.

Bridgeport, Conn. ______ 189__

Sold to

This c. 1890 billhead was used by the David Trubee and Company, wholesale grocers. The firm was one of numerous provision companies located on Water Street.

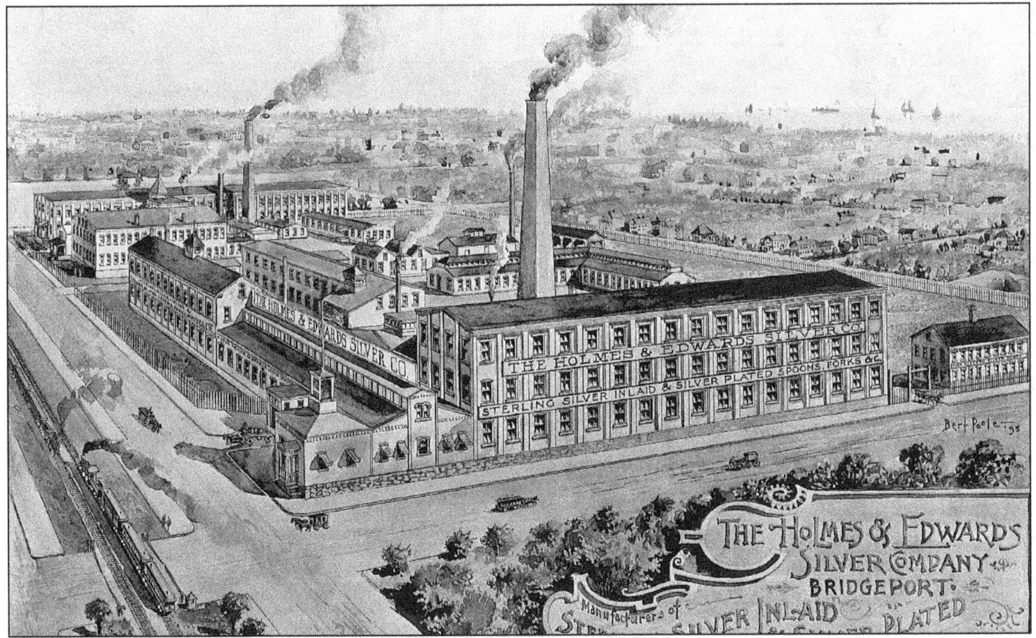

Holmes and Edwards Silver Company's guarantee was one that families all over the United States relied on—the company's flatware would last 25 years with ordinary family use. The company, founded in 1881 by Col. C. Holmes and George Edwards, moved their headquarters to Bridgeport c. 1888 to a factory on Seaview Avenue. The company conducted business all over the world, changing its name to the International Silver Company in the 1930s. Silver specialty items made by the company are highly prized by collectors today. This 1893 drawing shows Long Island Sound in the distance with sailboats.

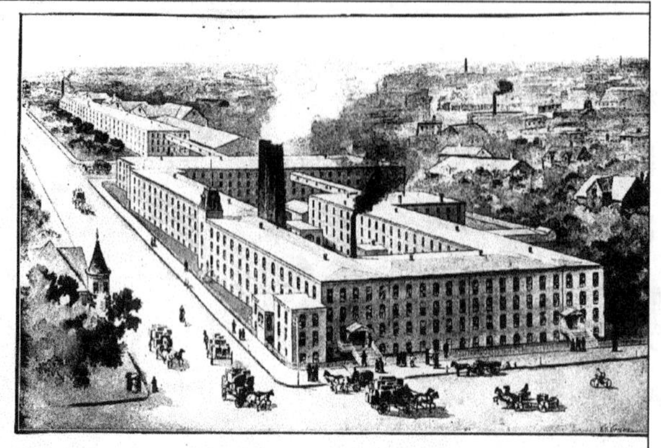

THE WARNER BROTHERS CO.

Factory extends from Lafayette Street across Warren Street to Myrtle Avenue, and from Atlantic Street to Gregory Street. The first building was erected in 1874. Present buildings give 200,000 square feet of floor space for manufacturing purposes. Over 2,000 hands employed.

REDFERN CORSETS

are boned with Greenland whalebone, and easily surpass in beauty and in perfection of style and fit any corsets made in America.

WARNER'S RUST-PROOF CORSETS

are boned with Rust-Proof and are sold in enormous quantities at popular prices. They are unique in being absolutely Rust-Proof, and in having the same care expended on their design and manufacture as is usually given only to high priced goods.

SECURITY RUBBER BUTTON HOSE SUPPORTERS

are also manufactured here. Other important departments are the Paper Box Department (one of the largest in New England), the Corset Wire and Clasp Department, the

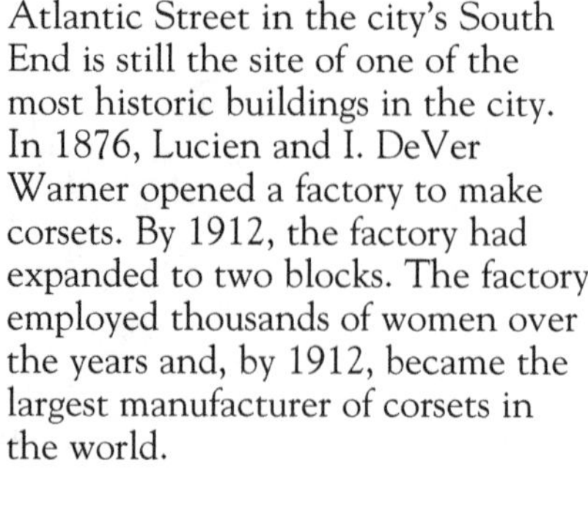

Atlantic Street in the city's South End is still the site of one of the most historic buildings in the city. In 1876, Lucien and I. DeVer Warner opened a factory to make corsets. By 1912, the factory had expanded to two blocks. The factory employed thousands of women over the years and, by 1912, became the largest manufacturer of corsets in the world.

Since the Warner Corset Company on Atlantic Street became one of the largest employers in the world, the Warner Brothers opened a facility to help educate and provide a social space for many of the young, immigrant female employees. On November 5, 1887, Mrs. Grover Cleveland attended the opening of the Seaside Institute, the first facility of its kind in the United States. The institute provided classes in bookkeeping, needlework, English, and sewing for women.

In October 1876, employees of the Warner Brothers factory gathered outside of the Atlantic and Lafayette Street building to have a photograph taken. While a few male employees are shown on the right, the company employed many females as seamstresses. Many of the women were very young and, as in this photograph, some were girls. Before child labor laws of the 20th century, children often worked in factories.

The Lake Torpedo Boat Company was opened in 1897 on Seaview Avenue. Simon Lake chose the location because it had a well-protected area for launching experimental crafts, as well as easy access to Long Island Sound and the Atlantic Ocean. Note the roller coaster of Pleasure Beach in the distance.

Bridgeport citizens became used to seeing submarines launched off Seaview Avenue. Simon Lake sometimes gave special invitations to ride inside one of the submarines, serving lunch to underwater spectators so they could say they had eaten underwater. Here is one of the many submarines that Lake launched in Bridgeport Harbor.

"The most modern and complete automobile plant in the country" is how advertisements described the Locomobile Company in the beginning of the 20th century. The plant, located at the foot of Main Street near Bridgeport harbor and Seaside Park, produced steam- and gas-powered automobiles, which were considered the most reliable and innovative automobiles of the time.

The Locomobile became a symbol of luxury in the American psyche. Producing only four cars a day in the plant, the company used the best materials: silver accessories by Tiffany, velvet and silk upholstery, and electric intercoms. Presidents and royalty purchased the car all over the world. Using extravagant advertising, the ornate advertisements featured every detail of the vehicles. Often photographs were taken of Locomobiles using the beauty of Seaside Park to emphasize the car's elegance and extravagance. This town model was designed and built for Elsie French Vanderbilt in 1916, shown here in Seaside Park.

Inventor Buckminster Fuller used the old Locomobile factory at the foot of Main Street to build one of the strangest cars ever designed, the Dymaxion. Fuller and his partner, Starling Burgess, a yacht designer, built the automobile as a sleek, three-wheeled vehicle that could run at a speed of 120 miles an hour. The designers showed the automobile at the 1933 World's Fair; however, lack of interest put the company out of business by 1935.

Igor Sikorsky's South Avenue plant, located in Bridgeport's South End had the first helicopter assembly line in the world. Igor Sikorsky designed his first helicopter in 1909 and frequently tested designs in the Bridgeport area. The inside of the South Avenue plant is seen here in 1944, with workers building the R-4B helicopter under often tight security. This photograph released by the war department was the first to be taken inside the plant.

Shown here is Buckley Brothers Fuel Terminal in 1956. This firm, founded in the 1930s, is located at the foot of Seaview Avenue on the former site of the Lake Torpedo Boat Company. Around the bend from Buckley Brothers, up on Johnson's Creek, are *Miamogue* and *East End*, two of the city's oldest yacht clubs. *Miamogue* was founded in 1905 and *East End* was founded in 1912.

Shown in this 1956 view are Cilco Terminal and Carpenter Steel, located on Seaview Avenue. Two freighters lie at the Cilco (City Lumber Company) wharf in the center of the photograph. The busy terminal, started by the Schine brothers in the 1930s, deals in the bulk shipment of lumber, steel, produce, and general cargo. To the left of Cilco is the Carpenter Steel factory, housed in buildings originally occupied by the American Tube and Stamping Company. This site has now been cleared to make way for the new Derecktors shipyard.

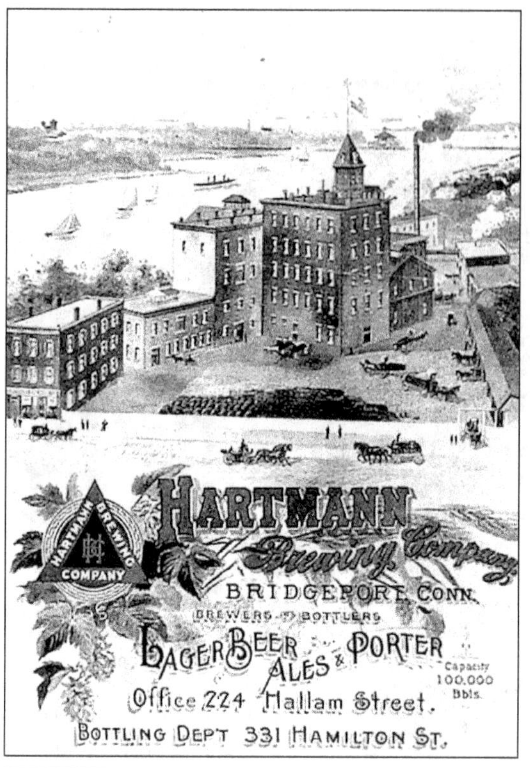

This romantic view of Bridgeport's Yellow Mill Pond, looking out to Long Island Sound, was used for advertising the Hartmann Brewing Company in East Bridgeport. Charles H. Hartmann was a brewer from Germany who started the company c. 1885 on Hallam Street. The company was sold to the Home Brewery, which eventually was sold and became the Bridgeport Brewery.

The Bridgeport

"The Motor That Motes"

THE BRIDGEPORT MOTOR CO. PORTLAND, ME., NOV. 12, 1907.

Gentlemen: During the past six years I have owned and operated three "Bridgeport" motors in the several boats I have had. Thinking it possible you would like to know of the performance of the 14 H. P. sold me two years ago, would advise that the motor was installed in a 30-foot cabin launch and turns a three blade 24-inch wheel with 38-inch pitch to advertised speed, driving the large hull better than ten miles an hour; run more than 2,000 miles in 1906 and fully 2,500 miles the past season with not one dollar for repairs since it was installed.

The boat is now out of commission, but a careful inspection of the motor in winter quarters, shows no signs of wear of any of the moving parts, and no repairs except paint needed for another.

The motor is the easiest to start of any I have ever seen, absolutely reliable in this respect. The compression after two seasons is perfect, as it starts by snapping the spark after the motor has been stopped several hours. It is also easy to control, as I can maintain speed from one to ten miles an hour. The engine is simplicity itself, with no trappy parts; all internal mechanism easy of access if repairs or adjustment should be necessary, and perfect in operation. My experience and observation justify me in saying, "owners of 'Bridgeports' are sailing while others are tinkering."

Yours very truly,
C. W. HANSON, Pres., AUG. P. FULLER CO.

The Bridgeport Motor Co. Inc.

BRIDGEPORT, CONN.

Stock Stores

New York, N. Y., BOWLER, HOLMES & HECKER CO., 141 Liberty Street

Boston, Mass. BRIDGEPORT MOTOR CO. 81 Central Wharf	Jersey City, N. J. BRUNS MOTOR EXCHANGE	Portland, Me. STOUGHTON-FOLKINS CO.

The September 1908 issue of *Motorboat* magazine featured this advertisement for the Bridgeport Motor Company. In the early 1900s, the manufacture of gasoline marine engines was a burgeoning industry in Bridgeport. In the same issue of *Motorboat*, three other Bridgeport firms—the Wolverine Motor Company, Bull Pup Motors, and the van Auken Motorworks—ran display advertisements touting their engines.

The tug *YT* tows the schooner *Ernestina* on Black Rock Harbor in 1989. The historic *Ernestina,* built in Gloucester, Massachusetts, in 1894, was a Grand Banks fisherman and arctic exploration vessel in its early days. It later engaged in the transatlantic Cape Verdean packet trade until 1982, when it was gifted by the Republic of Cape Verde to the people of the United States. It now operates as a sail-training vessel out of New Bedford, Massachusetts. Its close ties to Bridgeport's Cape Verdean community make it a popular visitor to the city.

Shipwrights stand before the newly completed hull of the HMS *Rose* in the spring of 1986. The *Rose*, a replica of an 18th-century British frigate, was towed to Black Rock Harbor in 1984. It arrived in badly deteriorated condition and a major restoration effort was soon launched. Over the next several years, it was rebuilt quite literally from "stem to stern" in the largest wooden boat construction project seen in Black Rock since the clipper ship era.

HMS *Rose* is shown at the Statue of Liberty/Op-Sail Celebration in New York Harbor, July 4, 1986. *Rose* joined tall ships from around the world at this memorable event. Over the next 14 years, the *Rose* visited hundreds of port cities on the East Coast, the Great Lakes, the Caribbean, and Europe in her dual role as a sail-training vessel and goodwill ambassador for the city of Bridgeport.

Four

LIGHTING OUR WAY

Fayerweather Lighthouse was built at the end of Fayerweather Island in 1823, replacing an earlier light knocked down during a great storm in 1821. Until 1851, when the first lighthouse was constructed off Bridgeport Harbor, it was the only beacon from Stratford Point to Norwalk. The light was in operation until 1933, when the U.S. Lighthouse Service discontinued its operation. In this 1905 view, the light's small oil house is seen to the right. The oil house, which held a supply of sperm whale oil for the light's eight lamps, was destroyed by vandals in the 1960s. In 1998, the light was completely restored with funding provided by the Black Rock Community Council and the City of Bridgeport.

Catherine Moore helped her father, Stephen Moore, with the light for many years after he became keeper of the Fayerweather Light in 1817. However, when Stephen fell ill, Catherine assumed the role of keeper of the Fayerweather Light. For 50 years she kept the light and, finally in 1871, was appointed officially by the U.S. government as the keeper of Fayerweather Light. Catherine continued the job, retiring in 1879. Catherine Moore was a legendary character in her day. Besides keeping the light and caring for her father and mother (both of whom lived until their 90s) for 54 years, she rescued 21 mariners from shipwreck, made a good living at oystering, and restored trees and vegetation lost to the storms, which frequently washed over the island. She also found time to carve duck decoys, which are highly prized by collectors today. To recognize Catherine Moore's heroism and her efforts as a pioneer conservationist, the Bridgeport Regional Aquaculture School research vessel, launched in 1994, was named in her honor.

Shown here is the lighthouse keeper's house on Fayerweather Island. Sitting on the porch with his assistants is head keeper Leonard Clark. The Gothic-style house was constructed by the U.S. Lighthouse Service in 1873 and was home to a number of keepers, including Stephen and Catherine Moore, Leonard Clark and wife Mary, and John D. Davis. When Fayerweather Light was taken out of service in 1933, caretakers occupied the house until it was destroyed by a fire in the 1970s.

Seen in this view are Fayerweather Lighthouse keepers Leonard and Mary E. Clark. During the Civil War, Leonard Clark was wounded at the Battle of the Wilderness. After being discharged from the U.S. Army, he went to sea, becoming captain of a whaling vessel for several years. Recurring pain from an old war injury forced him to give up his seagoing career. In 1879, he was appointed keeper of the Fayerweather Light, succeeding Catherine Moore. When Clark died in 1906, his wife, Mary, assumed his duties for the next two months until her replacement by John D. Davis.

March. 1 Light southerly wind, smoky.
2 N. E. to S. Cloudy.
3 Westerly wind, fresh.
4 N. W. blowing hard. Clear.
5 " " " " "
6 " " " " "
7 Blowing fresh. Wind W.
8 the same.
9 " "
10 Light and variable.
11 Wind N. E. snow.
12 Blowing very hard, N. W. Snow.
13 " " " " " "
14 Moderate and variable Clear.

This journal was written by Leonard Clark during his tenure as keeper at the Fayerweather Lighthouse (Black Rock Lighthouse). The journal is kept in the Historical Collections of the Bridgeport Public Library. The page shown here, from March 1888, documents Clark's weather observations, which he recorded on a daily basis. Note the entries for March 11–13, in which Clark notes, "wind N.E. snow" and "blowing very hard, N.W. snow." These are the dates of the Blizzard of 1888, in which Bridgeport and much of the Northeast were hit with more than two feet of snow and drifts that stood several feet high. Imagine being out in the lighthouse during that legendary storm!

The Bridgeport Lighthouse, shown here *c.* 1930, marked the entrance to Bridgeport Harbor. The federal government constructed the lighthouse in 1871 and reflected the dramatic increase in harbor activity. For a brief period, the Bridgeport Lighthouse was one of the nation's armed lights. During the Spanish-American War, a battery of 10-inch guns were installed to protect the harbor from Spanish warships. Just beyond the light is the ferryboat *Park City*, which operated between Bridgeport and Port Jefferson, Long Island. The lighthouse was demolished in 1953 after a fire.

Seaside Park and the Locomobile automotive plant, which was located just to the east of the waterfront park, were under close scrutiny during World War I. Tight security was set up at the plant as well as at other plants in the city to protect the important role that Bridgeport played in the Arsenal of Democracy. A military command post was erected in front of the Locomobile plant in 1917, directly in front of the Bridgeport lighthouse (barely visible on the right). A sentry was posted who patrolled with a bayoneted rifle, looking out onto the Sound for any unwelcome intruders.

The impetus for the construction of Penfield Lighthouse was the increasing shipping activity in Bridgeport Harbor after the Civil War. Penfield Reef jutted out perilously close to the route of steamers and schooners operating between Bridgeport and New York, and numerous vessels were lost or grounded as shipping traffic grew. In a petition presented to the House of Representatives on July 2, 1868, shipowners, captains, and pilots urged that Congress establish a light station at the outer part of the reef. Several options were considered, including the stationing of a lightship until the Second Empire, dwelling-tower style was chosen. According to legend, Penfield is haunted by the ghost of Fred Jordan, a keeper who drowned off the light in 1916.

Bridgeport's Tongue Point Light, affectionately known to locals as the "Bug Light," sits at the end of Tongue Point on the western shore of Bridgeport Harbor. The cast-iron conical light was constructed in 1894. Originally at the end of a breakwater that extended out into the harbor, the light was moved to its present location in 1921. The keeper of Tongue Point Lighthouse from 1949 to 1979 was Robert Baker, also keeper of the Bridgeport Lighthouse in the early 1950s. In this c. 1947 photograph taken by Bridgeport Post's Frank Decerbo, the ferryboat *Brinkerhoff* steams past the light toward Pleasure Beach.

Raymond Keefe and friends are seen here out for a day cruise on the Sound *c.* 1930. In the background is Middleground Lighthouse. This light warns mariners from the Stratford Shoals, which lie about six miles southeast from Bridgeport. Construction began on the lighthouse in 1876 and was completed, with great hardship, in 1878.

From the late 1790s to the 1980s, lightships were stationed along America's coastline to guide ships past dangerous rocks and shoals. Four lightships were once stationed in Long Island Sound, the closest at Stratford Shoals. The largest and most famous of the lightships built in the country is the *Nantucket* No. 112. At its anchorage 42 miles southeast of Nantucket Island, it warned vessels off the treacherous Nantucket shoals from 1936 to 1975. It replaced an earlier lightship, the *Nantucket* No. 117, which was rammed and sunk by the RMS *Olympic* in 1934. Since the *Nantucket* No. 112 was often the first glimpse of U.S. territory seen by immigrants arriving from Europe, it was known as the "Statue of Liberty of the Sea." In 1997, *Nantucket* No. 112 was donated by the Intrepid Air Space Museum to the HMS *Rose* Foundation. A designated national historic landmark, it is now on display at Captain's Cove Seaport on Black Rock Harbor. This 1997 photograph, taken by noted aerial photographer Morgan Kaolian, shows the lightship entering Black Rock Harbor.

Five

Moving on the Sound

The lucky winners of a contest sponsored by the Bridgeport Post are shown boarding the steamer *William G. Payne* for a day trip to New York. The *William G. Payne*, later renamed *Bridgeport*, was one of the last side-wheelers built for the Sound. Some called it "the fastest side-wheeler in America."

BRIDGEPORT STEAMBOAT CO.

(Lessees People's Steamboat Co.)

TIME TABLE.

JAMES H. JENKINS, PRESIDENT.
F. H. CONNELLY, SUPERINTENDENT.

Gift of Tom Hurley
of "Bart" Hurley Estate

Steamer Rosedale,

Leaves Bridgeport at 7:30 A. M.
Arrives 31st Street, 11:00 A. M.
" Pier 39, 11:15 A. M.

RETURNING.

Leaves New York, Pier 39,
Foot of Market St.
3:00 P. M.
" " " E. 31st Street.
3:15 P M.
Arrives Bridgeport, 6:45 P. M.

On Saturdays Boat leaves One Hour Earlier.

Fare, - - - - - 50c.
Excursion Tickets, Good until used. 75c.

Freight taken at very lowest rates.
Western Freight taken from Bridgeport at New York Rates and Bills of Lading given.

Shown here is a timetable for the steamer *Rosedale*. The *Rosedale* operated from Bridgeport to New York's Pier 39. Note the fare was only 50¢, with 75¢ for excursion fare.

The SS *Rosedale* traveled daily from Bridgeport to New York City from the years 1879 to 1904. Capt. John Smith brought the steamer *Rosedale* to Bridgeport, managing the steam line. P.T. Barnum was one of the stockholders of Smith's company. Steamship business was very competitive on Long Island Sound.

The *Nutmeg State* was built by the Bridgeport Steamboat Company in 1890 to replace the old *Waterbury*. On a trip from Bridgeport to New York on the morning of October 14, 1899, the ship caught fire near Execution Light, forcing Capt. Charles Brooks to beach it near Sands Point, New York. The fire eventually ignited its cargo of textiles and the vessel burned to the water's edge. As a result of the swift action of Captain Brooks, all of its 60 passengers were evacuated safely. Seven crewmen, however, died while fighting the fire.

The steamer *Richard Peck* was known as the "Greyhound of the Sound." It was a common sight off Bridgeport as it plied its route from New Haven to New York and back. The trip each way was just over four hours. This oil painting of the *Peck* was done by F.H. Ward for his former captain, Theodore Witherwax. It now hangs in the Bridgeport Public Library.

The Bridgeport and Port Jefferson Steamboat Company has operated a cross-sound ferry service without interruption since 1883. Its first vessel, the *Nonwantuc*, was replaced by the durable *Park City*, built in Port Jefferson in 1898. The firm added a second vessel, the *Long Island*, in 1924. The *Park City*, shown here embarking passengers at Port Jefferson c. 1910, was altered in 1921 to transport automobiles as well as walk-on traffic. A new *Park City* now sails the cross-sound route along with the *Grand Republic* (1968) and the *P.T. Barnum*, launched in 1999.

This is a view looking east from the Stratford Avenue Bridge c. 1950. The old steamer *Catskill*, built in 1922, sits at the Bridgeport and Port Jefferson Steamboat Company terminal, then located just beyond the bridge. The small fishing dragger *Eda* lies just in front of the terminal. She supplied Sorrentino's fish market by the bridge. Just beyond the ferryboat is the former United Illuminating plant.

Built at Bath, Maine, in 1923, the *Martha's Vineyard II* was one of four steel-hulled steamers commissioned by the New York, New Haven, and Hartford Railroad Company in the 1920s. It was originally christened *Islander* and, with its sister ships, ferried passengers back and forth from the mainland to Nantucket and the vineyard. This route was quite lucrative, since air service to the islands had not yet been established. *Martha's Vineyard* was acquired by the Bridgeport and Port Jefferson Steamboat Company in 1968, replacing the old *Catskill*. *Martha's Vineyard* in turn was superseded by the *Grand Republic*, which can accommodate 1,000 passengers and 82 vehicles.

Bridgeporters will remember this former terminal for the Bridgeport and Port Jefferson Ferry. This May 1960 photograph shows a line of cars heading west into the city.

Members of the Bridgeport chapter of the Kiwanis Club gathered on the steamer *City of Brockton* on August 16, 1917. Men of the club sailed in Bridgeport's harbor listening to Shaw's orchestra, while eating a New England–style dinner. The steamer is in motion in this photograph—notice the flapping flags.

Six

Enjoying the Sound

The Park City Yacht Club, founded in 1890, was the oldest boating organization in the city. The group's first meeting place was the old Robbin's shipyard building on East Main Street. In 1897, construction was completed on the club's new headquarters, located where the Yellow Mill once stood. The club flourished as a rendezvous spot for local yachtsmen until the early 1930s, when dwindling membership and encroachment by nearby industry forced its closure.

Park City Yacht Club was located on the Yellow Mill Pond on the site of a mill first established by Joseph Walker in 1792. This view shows the clubhouse on the southeast end of the Yellow Mill Bridge.

The Bridgeport Yacht Club was located along Anchorage Drive on the Black Rock Harbor shore. The three-story structure was built in 1898 and replaced the club's old headquarters on Bridgeport Harbor. Its members maintained a large fleet of private yachts, including the famous racing schooner *Atlantic*. Visiting yachts included Cornelius Vanderbilt's *Rainbow* and August Belmont's *Mineola*. By World War I, the club had disbanded and the naval reserve took over occupation of the building. Finally, in 1923, the old clubhouse was demolished except for two sections, which were salvaged and converted into private dwellings.

On June 30, 1900, Marion and Edward Holmes set out from Oyster Bay, Long Island, on a three-month cruise along the New England coast. They sailed aboard the yacht *Privateer*, recently acquired by Capt. R.A.C. Smith from William Randolph Hearst. For a week in July, the *Privateer* stopped at Black Rock Harbor where Captain Smith, Marion and Edward Holmes, and the rest of their party were the guests of the Bridgeport Yacht Club.

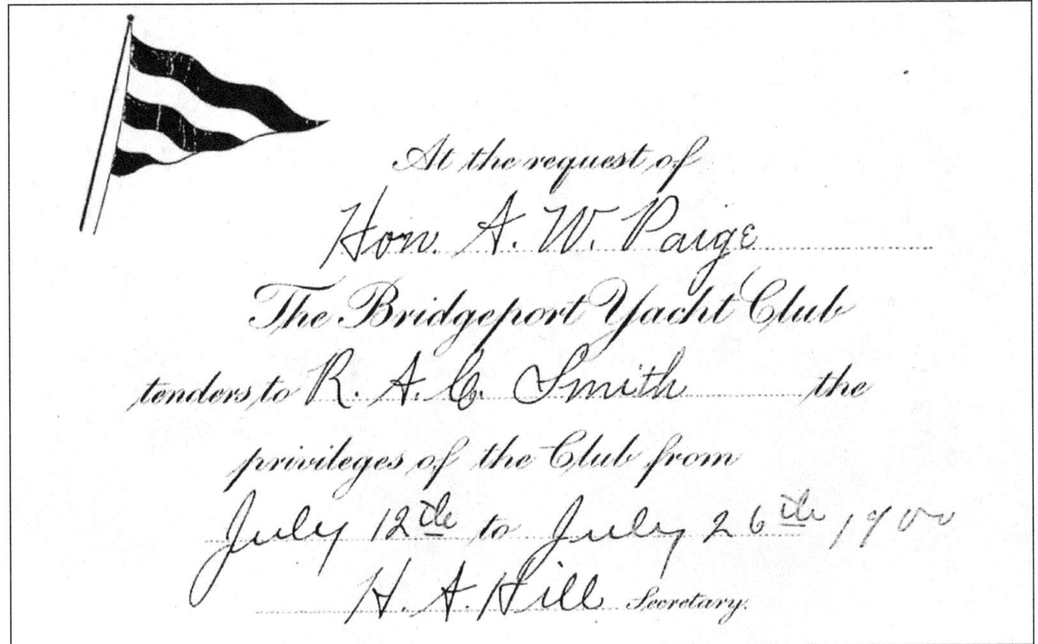

At the request of
Hon. A. W. Paige
The Bridgeport Yacht Club
tenders to R. A. C. Smith the
privileges of the Club from
July 12th to July 26th 1900
H. A. Hill Secretary.

By this invitation, Commo. A.W. Paige extends the privileges of the Bridgeport Yacht Club to Capt. R.A.C. Smith of the *Privateer*. After the demise of the Bridgeport Yacht Club, a new group, the Black Rock Yacht Club and Lawn Club, took over the old club's charter. Black Rock Yacht Club remains one of the most active yachting organizations on the Sound. It still retains the parent club's original pennant, seen here on the invitation.

Seen here are Mr. and Mrs. William B. Leonard aboard the yacht *Privateer* off Bridgeport in July 1900. This photograph, found in the log of the *Privateer*, came with a notation that read, "W.B. Leonard looking for the Fayerweather Lighthouse."

Shown here is a view of yachting on Bridgeport Harbor *c.* 1910. Beyond the small powerboat, several schooners lie at anchor. The Locomobile plant can be seen in the distance on the west side of the harbor.

The Lehmann Shore House was located near the foot of Seaview Avenue, close to the Lake Torpedo Boat Company. It was opened in 1891 by Otto Lehmann, who learned his trade as a chef aboard transatlantic steamers. The establishment gained wide repute for its shore dinners and was a favorite with local politicians and captains of industry.

This view shows a summer day on the George Hotel pier *c.* 1900. Swimming was promoted in the hotel brochure, which offered springboards and diving boards for those of "great natatorial accomplishment." For the more timid, wheeled "bathing houses," which lowered swimmers gradually into the water, were provided.

The renowned George Hotel opened along Grover's Hill on Black Rock Harbor in 1874. It was built by and named for George A. Wells, an associate of P.T. Barnum. The hotel's five-story main building, shown here, had 106 rooms, all equipped with gas lighting, forced-air heating, and running water. The hotel offered visitors seven 20-room cottages on its extensive grounds. Two piers accommodated steamers and visiting yachtsmen. An 1888 brochure describes the visit of the Atlantic Yacht Club and points out that "among our present guests are the representative families of New York, Brooklyn, Philadelphia, St. Louis, New Orleans, etc." The George Hotel operated until *c.* 1900, when the main building was moved by barge up to the harbor to the West End. A number of the old cottages and the Shore House, now occupied by the Black Rock Yacht Club, remain on the former grounds of the hotel.

The vessels *Meta*, *Anita*, and *Stella* wrecked near the Shore House of the old George Hotel (now the Black Rock Yacht Club building) after a July 1893 hurricane. In an interview with the *New York World* magazine in 1889, lighthouse keeper Kate Moore related, "Sometimes there were more than two hundred sailing vessels in here at night, and some nights there were as many as three or four wrecks so you may judge how essential it was that they see our light."

The Black Rock Yacht Club is shown here after the Hurricane of 1938. The club's location near the mouth of Black Rock Harbor makes it vulnerable to southerlies coming off the Sound.

Members of the Black Rock Yacht Club juniors prepare posters for the Bermuda Shorts Dance in July 1955.

The Commodore Henry A. Bishop Cup predicted log race has been a tradition for powerboat skippers of the Miamogue, Pequonnock, East End, and Fayerweather Yacht Clubs since 1910. The race was founded by Henry A. Bishop, commodore of the old Bridgeport Yacht Club. Shown making preparations for the race are James P. Hoyt of Pequonnock, Keith B. Soller of East End, and Albert Stead of Miamogue.

Shown in 1959 is the Pequonnock Yacht Club headquarters at the foot of California Street. Pequonnock was first organized in 1906 and played an important part in the early development of yachting in Bridgeport Harbor. The club's original charter and purpose was "to encourage boat building and aquatic sports, especially sailing and rowing, to promote naval architecture and the cultivation of marine science and knowledge; to establish and maintain a meeting place for its members." The clubhouse pictured here was built in 1912. Although threatened by a major redevelopment project in the lower East Main Street area, Pequonnock still maintains an active presence in the harbor. On the right is the old Bridgeport–Port Jefferson Ferry Terminal dock.

California Street is shown *c.* 1947. The large building on the left houses the Hitchcock Gas Engine Company, originally located on Seaview Avenue near the Lake Torpedo Boat Company. Hitchcock's has been operated by the Brown family for nearly a century. On the far right is the still active Peqonnock Yacht Club. Just beyond Pequonnock was Pixley's Boatyard, now the home of the MOVE Yacht Club.

Kaye and Noel Williams are shown aboard Kaye's first vessel, a kayak that he built on Fayerweather Island. Just across the harbor in Black Rock is Fayerweather Yacht Club, founded *c.* 1919. The club, which is still active today, is quartered in the old Black Rock customs house, built in 1772. Kaye Williams grew up to found Captain's Cove Seaport, just up the harbor from this scene.

Shown here is the headquarters of the Fayerweather Yacht Club in 1932. Increasing membership led the club to purchase the nearby former customs house in 1937.

Seen in this *c.* 1908 view are boats hauled at the foot of Brewster Street. This small yard is still used for boat storage by the Fayerweather Yacht Club.

Mayor Hugh Curran signs an agreement to lease city waterfront property to the MOVE Yacht Club in October 1971. The club is located at the foot of California Street, on the former site of the old Pixley boatyard. Signing and witnessing the agreement are, from left to right, the following: (front row) Hayward Frye, Mayor Curran, and Victoria P. Raines; (back row) George C. Scott and Joseph W. Raines.

Irving Cone pilots his new Chris Craft on Black Rock Harbor *c.* 1960. Up to 200 pleasure boats moor in Black Rock during the summer season.

Captain's Cove Seaport was founded by ex-commercial lobsterman Kaye Williams in 1982. The facility has become a hub of marine activity in Black Rock Harbor. Captain's Cove has been the home of the tall ships HMS *Rose*, *Black Pearl*, and the *John E. Pfriem* and host to numerous annual fundraisers and waterfront events. Also located at the Captain's Cove are the historic lightship *Nantucket* and the Dundon House Maritime Museum. Adjacent to the seaport is the Bridgeport Regional Aquaculture School, opened in 1992. On its four-acre campus, the school offers hundreds of local high school students training in marine trades. Those students with a particular interest in marine biology attend classes aboard the *Catherine Moore*, the school's 56-foot research vessel, launched in 1994.

In June 1892, announcements were made that owners of the beach, McMahon and Wren, had hired a manager to run the entire "island" they called "Pleasure Beach." Pleasure Beach is actually a barrier island off the shore of the city's Newfield area. A large theater was built that could house 600 people, and the bathing beach was improved. The steamer *Lenoir* took passengers over hourly from Seaview Avenue.

Yearly, a multipaged booklet would be printed showing the current year's activities for Pleasure Beach. In 1897, this booklet showed the various highlights at the park: the best bicycle track in all of New England, fine swimming, baseball games, and the annual baby contest.

In 1904, George Tilyou, the developer of Coney Island in New York took over the management of Pleasure Beach, changing the name to Steeplechase Island after a popular amusement ride in the park. This 1908 photograph shows the penny arcade (left) and the carousel. Other popular rides of the time included the Ferris wheel, the figure-eight roller coaster, and the huge water toboggan ride.

Fires were a common occurrence at Pleasure Beach over the years. In this *c.* 1908 photograph, a fire is burning near the bicycle track at Steeplechase Island. The remote location of Pleasure Beach made it difficult for fire trucks to make it out to the island to extinguish fires in time, so the amusement park had its own water pumps available. A fire in 1953 was started by bad wiring, destroying concessions, the penny arcade, and the fun house. On June 16, 1996, the Pleasure Beach Bridge burned, making it impossible for motorists to reach the island.

The old chain ferry, shown here, transported passengers across the creek from Seaview Avenue to Steeplechase Island (Pleasure Beach). The ferry was taken out of service after the new Pleasure Beach bridge opened in May 1927.

A busy Fourth of July weekend in 1939 has people lined up at the entrance to Pleasure Beach. It was common for local factories and schools to have regular annual outings to the park.

Electric Cars Direct to New Ferry Line
Foot Seaview Avenue Every 5 Minutes.

DELIGHTFUL SHORE DINNERS.

Pleasure Beach Cafe.

. . BILL OF FARE. . .

Steamed Soft Clams, 25c.; Little Neck Clams, on Half Shell per doz. 25c.; Steamed Little Neck Clams, 50c.; Clam Roast, 50c.; Clam Chowder, 20c.; Clam Fritters, 50c.; Fried Clams, 50c.; Broiled Blue Fish, 40c.; Spanish Mackerel, 50c.; Broiled Weak Fish, 40c.; Fried Eels, 50c.; Broiled Split Eels, 50c.; Soft Shell Crabs, 50c.; Broiled Lobster, 50c.; Cold Boiled Lobster, 50c.; Lobster Salad, 50c.; Tea and Coffee, per cup, 10c.; Whole Broiled Spring Chicken, $1.25; Half Broiled Spring Chicken, 75c.; Watermelon, 15c.; Ice Cream, 10c.

SHORE DINNER, 8 Courses with Vegetables, $1.00
With Chicken, $1.25.

Shore Dinners Ordered by Telephone
Served upon arrival at the Beach Cafe.

A restaurant on the island called Pleasure Beach Cafe advertised its menu in the 1897 booklet. The restaurant specialized in shore dinners, which consisted of an eight-course meal having the best of New England seafood. The entire eight-course dinner, with vegetables, cost only $1.

This photograph of the inside of Pleasure Beach was taken by Lew Corbit in 1939. On the right are the arcades, while the roller coaster is in the background.

People today might think that rides were not very sophisticated in 1939, but here is a photograph of the very popular water ride at Pleasure Beach. Imagine the fun on a hot summer day of splashing along the water ride. The roller coaster, one of the highest in New England, is shown in the background. Many of these rides rival some of today's amusement park rides.

Any kid growing up in the Bridgeport area during the decades before the park closed remembers going to Kiddie Land at the Pleasure Beach park. A merry-go-round, Twirl-A-Whirl, and a miniature Ferris wheel were just some of the many rides that thrilled younger children who came to the park in 1939 and throughout the years. The area known as Kiddie Land had youngsters lining up again and again.

The ballroom at Pleasure Beach was known for its swinging times, especially during the 1930s and 1940s when top musicians like the Tommy Reynolds Orchestra, Gene Krupa, or Benny Goodman performed at the ballroom. "Krupa," a reporter quipped in the paper, "had enough [drums] to drive the entire city of Bridgeport to self destruction." Many local couples tell stories of first meeting at the Pleasure Beach ballroom.

Every year, the carousel horses would be carefully refurbished, so the works of art gleamed for the eyes of the public on opening day. The popular carousel was a tradition for young and old to ride. The original carousel horses are now on display at the Beardsley Park Carousel Pavilion.

Management of Steeplechase went back to the city after George Tilyou's death and a series of bad managers. On Memorial Day in 1938, the City of Bridgeport officially opened Pleasure Beach as a municipally operated facility. At a city employees' outing in the park in 1938, Mayor Jasper McLevy (center) talks to welfare commissioner Philip Magil (left) and public works director Pete Brewster. More than 30,000 people attended the park on the first day.

In 1941, some 600 city employees and their friends attended an annual outing to Pleasure Beach. From left to right are Irving H. Johnson, chairman of the drum corps competition; Frank "Shorty" Long of the welfare department, chairman of the picnic; Mayor Jasper McLevy; and Rev. Zolton Kish, director of the fife and drum corps of St. Stephen's School.

This 1955 aerial view of Pleasure Beach was taken by Corbit Studios. Most evident is the roller coaster on the left and the dance pavilion on the right. The white sandy beaches are also clearly visible.

During World War II, Mayor Jasper McLevy (left) and city officials inspect a police department bomb taxi at Pleasure Beach in a practice session. The city had to make sure it could safely defuse bombs that might be planted in factories and other areas of the city. Seaview Avenue is visible in the distance.

One of the events of the Barnum Festival of 1949 was set up in Pleasure Beach park to highlight local businesses in Bridgeport. The June exposition showed diverse products like washing machines, automobiles, and even tires.

Bridgeport Brass, whose president Herman Steinkraus founded the Barnum Festival, had one of the largest and most impressive displays of products, including a cowboy (right) made of brass. The Bridgeport Progress Exposition was held June 7–14, 1949.

Originally a club for people interested in horses, the Seaside Club changed its focus with the dawn of the automobile age—it became a social club. The club started in 1884, meeting in some rooms of Main Street. In 1891, this building on Lafayette Street became the Seaside Club's permanent home. When the club moved out, the Bridgeport Times-Star newspaper used this building for offices.

The Seaside Club expanded its activities to open a meetinghouse closer to the water. Organizing the Seaside Outing Club in 1894, members used this building on the east shore of Yellow Mill Pond on Seaview Avenue. It had a beautiful vista with a large inviting porch that looked out into Long Island Sound.

An unusual hobby for one Bridgeport resident was to take a piece of swampy wasteland on Bridgeport's East End near Newfield Park and transform it into a grass-carpeted, flower-decorated park. Civil War veteran W.P. Jessup devoted years of his life to planting and working to make this lot on Seaview Avenue and Adams Street a quiet oasis in the city. Jessup lived on Adams Street. He took the land that was once part of the James O'Rourke estate and began to plant trees, roses, and grass. Nearby children at Newfield School would plant trees in the new park every Arbor Day. Jessup, who served in the Civil War at Gettysburg, lived until 1939, 96 years old at his death. The park, located just a stone's throw from the water, was taken over by the city in 1939.

The 100th anniversary of Newfield Park was celebrated in 1998, a park in Bridgeport's East End that has seen its share of baseball over the years. James O'Rourke, who grew up on a farm at the very site, learned to play baseball in the fields of the East End, long before it was developed into city neighborhoods. O'Rourke played professional baseball for Boston and other teams, and it was his dream to open a baseball ground in Bridgeport, on the land his family owned where he first played ball. On May 13, 1898, James O'Rourke managed the Bridgeport Orators against Springfield of the Eastern League at the new baseball grounds called Newfield, right on his family's farmland. Bridgeport lost the game but gained a baseball field! James O'Rourke is pictured here (left) with his son, who also played ball, James "Queenie" O'Rourke.

Shown here is Newfield Park in the city's East End during World War I. Hundreds of residents came to the park this cold day to watch the Home Guard marching in the park. Residents are sitting in the stands on the left field line.

The easternmost edge of Seaside Park, shown in 1888, had a bathing area and buildings used for changing rooms, some cottages, and refreshment stands. One building was even set up as a temporary photographic studio by some local enterprising photographer. This area was eventually the site of the Locomobile plant and is currently occupied by Remington Products.

The 17th Connecticut Volunteer Regiment camped in Seaside Park in 1862. Practicing maneuvers in the large areas near the water, the regiment was lead by Col. William Noble, just days before leaving for battle. In 1867, the regiment posed together in the park for this reunion photograph, only a year after park commissioners officially authorized funds for the development of Seaside Park.

In 1892, a huge celebration took place to honor Columbus's landing in America. Hundreds of residents lined the shores of Seaside Park to witness a ceremony that had A.H. Davis assuming the role of Christopher Columbus, while the harbormaster, Capt. John McNeil, stretched his arm out in greeting, carefully negotiating a plank on the rocky shores of Long Island Sound.

Seaside Park was planned out carefully by the foremost landscape architects of the day: Frederick Law Olmsted and Calvert Vaux, designers of Central Park in New York. It was P.T. Barnum who inspired other residents—such as Capt. John Brooks, Capt. Burr Knapp, and Gen. William Noble—to give land to make a marine rural park, the first of its kind in the United States. This photograph was taken *c.* 1910 by T.S. Bronson, courtesy of the New Haven Colony Historical Society.

In October 1918, the Perry Memorial Arch was placed at the Park Avenue entrance to Seaside Park. Built of Vermont granite, the arch was designed by Henry Bacon, designer of the Lincoln Memorial in Washington, D.C., as a memorial to William Perry, former superintendent of the Wheeler and Wilson Sewing Machine Company.

Members of the Bridgeport Wheel Club, a bicycle club from the beginning of the 20th century, pose in front of the Barnum Statue in Seaside Park. Men raced their bicycles at tracks at Pleasure Beach and Seaside Park and in competition throughout the region. P.T. Barnum posed for this statue, sculpted by artist Thomas Ball. Kept under wraps when it was finished in 1888, the statue was finally placed by Barnum's family and friends in Seaside Park after Barnum's death in 1891.

Hundreds of people went down to Seaside Park every summer to enjoy the beach. This *c.* 1917 postcard shows the beach just after the bathhouse was built. The July 29, 1887 issue of the *Bridgeport Standard* stated, "Sea bathing is now at its height and Bridgeport is favored as very few cities are—10 minutes from the center of the city brings one to Seaside Park, where [in the] afternoon may be seen thousands of men, women and children disporting themselves in the comfortable waters of the sound." At the time, saltwater was thought to have recuperative powers, bringing health and energy to ill people. The red-roofed bathhouse building on the right (designed by architect Ernest Southey) was also used for dances.

Elias Howe Jr. obtained a patent for the first practical sewing machine in 1845. In 1865, Howe opened a sewing machine factory on the East Side of Bridgeport, where as many as 400 machines were manufactured a day. One of the first Bridgeport men to enlist in the Civil War, Elias Howe organized the 17th Connecticut Volunteers, serving as a private in Company D of the 17th. However, due to poor health, Howe never saw combat. Howe died in 1867, leaving his son Simon in charge of the Bridgeport factory.

P.T. Barnum provided money in his own will for a monument to be placed in Seaside Park in honor of Henry Bergh, the founder of the Society for Prevention of Cruelty to Animals. Although Bergh and Barnum eventually became friends, Henry Bergh had once sued Barnum, complaining of his treatment of circus animals. The monument was erected in 1897.

This amusing illustration appeared in the *Bridgeport Post* on February 28, 1918. The caption read, "This is the Soldiers and Sailors Monument at Seaside Park as it would appear if the Germans should capture Bridgeport. Don't let this happen. Buy War Savings Stamps with every available cent."

The Soldiers and Sailors Monument was erected by the Ladies Aid Society in 1876 to commemorate the Civil War dead. The statue was erected at the highest point of land in Seaside Park, making it a focal point to take photographs of the park. Often the statue is used as a backdrop for photographs. Here, soldiers decorate the monument during World War I.

Members of the Rambling Wheelmen Bicycle Club pose in front of the Soldiers and Sailors Monument after a day in the park. The bicycle club often raced at the Pleasure Beach track and sometimes rode at Seaside Park.

The 1925 Park City Giants pose against the Soldiers and Sailors Monument. Edward Bridgeforth is seated on the far left in the back row. Manager Bobby Green is pictured in the jacket and tie in the back row.

On July 4, 1917, soldiers raise a flag near the Spanish cannon. Photographs were taken of the local soldiers during World War I as they prepared throughout the city before they were shipped off to Europe.

This cannon arrived by train in 1900, having last been used in the Battle of Santiago in the Spanish-American War. When it was first placed in the southeast corner forming Point Lookout, two piles of cannon balls were placed near the cannon. The cannon balls have since disappeared. Often people sit on the cannon for a photograph, as these women did *c.* 1920. This photograph is from the Charles Callahan estate.

In 1917, it became a common sight for soldiers to practice maneuvers in Seaside Park, getting ready for World War I. Drilling and marching took place throughout the large expanse of the park.

Throughout the years, people often camped out in tents under the trees at Seaside Park. Here, however, soldiers set up camp trying to prepare themselves for similar conditions that they might find when they were shipped to Europe.

Singer sewing machines, the D.M. Read Company, and Warner Brothers were just a few of the familiar names displayed in the park as revered products of 1925 in the Bridgeport Progress Exposition. Jenkins Valves, located in the city's South End, proudly displayed the brass valves that made the company famous. Local newspapers pointed out that the exhibits clearly showed how Bridgeport earned the name "the Industrial Capital of Connecticut."

Bridgeport's many products were highlighted in a week-long exposition held in Seaside Park the week of May 30–June 6, 1925. Although the weather was terrifically hot, crowds of residents and visitors to the Park City crowded the exhibits. From fashion to valves, companies of Bridgeport displayed in booths their most-prized products. The tents were set up near the Park Avenue entrance to the park.

In this view of the 1962 reviewing stand, parade officials and crowds wait for the next float to appear in the Barnum Festival Parade. Early parades started out in Seaside Park, ending up in the Bulls Head section of the city. Over the years, however, the parade route has changed. Most years it started out in Seaside Park.

A float starts its way through the arch at Park Avenue, finding its way on the northern route of the 1952 Barnum Festival Parade. Crowds lined the streets up and down Park Avenue eagerly waiting for the next float. Photographers loved to use the Perry Memorial Arch as a backdrop for the floats as they made their entrance down the parade route.

At the 1950 Barnum Festival are, from left to right, Herman Steinkraus, 1950 ringmaster and Barnum Festival founder; Bill Hope, 1949 ringmaster; and University of Bridgeport president Jim Halsey on board with friends in Bridgeport's harbor on a cruise. Portside is Gertrude Birkmaier, Ethel Beckwith (the Herald), and Marjorie Heuschkel. On the starboard side are Mrs. Jerry Lineburgh, the Herald's society editor Ann Bridge, and Mrs. John A. Lyddy.

Bibliography

Brilvitch, Charles. *Walking through History, the Seaports of Black Rock and Southport.* Farfield, Connecticut: Fairfield Historical Society, 1977.

Clifford, Mary Louise and J. Candace Clifford. *Women Who Kept the Lights.* Williamsburg, Virginia: Cypress Communitations, 1993.

Danenberg, Elsie Nicholas. *The Story of Bridgeport.* Bridgeport, Connecticut: Bridgeport Centennial, 1936.

Foster, George H., Peter C. Weiglin. *Splendor Sailed the Sound.* San Mateo, California: Potentials Group Inc., 1989.

Grimaldi, Lennie. *Only in Bridgeport: An Illustrated History of the Park City.* 1st ed. Northridge, California: Windsor Publications, 1986. 2nd ed., Harbor Publishing, 1993.

Hamilton, Harlan. *Lights and Legends: A Historical Guide to Lighthouses of Long Island Sound, Fishers Island Sound and Block Island Sound.* Stamford, Connecticut: Westcott Cove Publishing Company, 1987.

Jones, Dick, ed. *Black Rock: A Bicentennial Picture Book.* Bridgeport, Connecticut: Black Rock Civic and Businessmen's Club Inc., 1976.

Justinius, Dr. Ivan O. *History of Black Rock.* Bridgeport, Connecticut: Bridgeport Black Rock Civic and Businessmen's Club, Inc., 1955.

Kochiss, John M. *Oystering from New York to Boston.* Middletown, Connecticut: Mystic Seaport Publishing, 1974.

Orcutt, Samuel. *The History of the Old Town of Stratford and the City of Bridgeport.* New Haven, Connecticut: Tuttle, Morehouse and Taylor, 1886.

Palmquist, David W. *Bridgeport: A Pictorial History.* Virginia Beach, 1981.

Waldo, George W. *Standard's History of Bridgeport.* The Standard Association, 1897.

Witkowski, Mary K. "From the Historical Collections," weekly column in the *Bridgeport News.*

Note: Newspaper clippings from local newspapers such as the *Bridgeport Post* (*Connecticut Post*) and the *Bridgeport Herald* were used. These are available on microfilm in the Bridgeport Public Library and in folders.

Index

www.ingramcontent.com/pod-product-compliance
Lightning Source LLC
LaVergne TN
LVHW081531100826
845153LV00004B/250

* 9 7 8 1 5 3 1 6 0 5 3 2 2 *